THE MONEY JAR

Save Your Way To Financial Freedom

GRANT SYLVESTER

Introduction by Bob Proctor

KEY PORTER BOOKS

Canadian Cataloguing in Publication Data

Sylvester, Grant.
The money jar

ISBN 1-55013-226-1

1. Finance, Personal. I. Title.

HG179.S95 1990 332.024 C89-095263-9

Typesetting: Alphabets
Printed and bound in Canada

Key Porter Books Limited
70 The Esplanade
Toronto, Ontario
Canada M5E 1R2

90 91 92 93 5 4 3 2 1

Contents

Acknowledgments / v
Introduction by Bob Proctor / vii
Foreword / 1
1 The Only Way to Financial Independence / 3
2 Ingredients in the Money Jar Recipe / 13
3 The First Secret of Financial Freedom / 21
4 The Second Secret of Financial Freedom / 25
5 Money Management: An Emotional Experience / 33
6 Saving: The Foundation of Your Financial Plan / 45
7 Spending: The Ultimate Seduction / 71
8 Investing Your Savings: Divide and Conquer / 79
9 RRSPs: The Most Misunderstood Savings Device / 91
10 Job Security: A Myth / 115
11 Inflation: The Enemy That Never Sleeps / 133
12 Government: Your Unwanted Planning Partner / 145
13 Life Insurance: Cornerstone of a Financial Plan / 153
14 Disability: The Crippling Facts / 171
15 Putting It All Together / 185
16 Where Do You Turn for Help? / 195
17 It's Never Too Late to Start / 205
Appendix / 213

Acknowledgments

I would like to dedicate this book to my family: Olga, Rob, Terry and Danny. I love them all. Their zest for "the good life" prompts me to provide for them as well as I can. In fact, it constantly amazes me to find that I am able to provide just a bit more than they can spend. They are an ongoing financial challenge.

I am particularly grateful to John D. Millyard, the master wordsmith whose inexhaustible hard work and patience made this book possible. As a result he now could easily qualify for a second (actually third) career as a financial planner.

Thank you to the officers, staff, financial-planning-center presidents and account executives of Money Concepts who share a dream with me of creating an innovative, exciting and vibrant new service for the Canadian public.

Thanks also to the thousands of clients of mine and of Money Concepts everywhere, who have taught me better than I have taught them. They are making my dreams come true by making their own dreams come true.

I owe a debt in the form of a deep regard that I can never fully repay, to Bob Proctor, whose unparalleled teaching abilities and genuine friendship have provided an underlying core of support to my life and my venture into independent business.

Finally, but certainly not least, a special thank you to the late Monsignor Athol "Pere" Murray and the Hounds of Notre Dame of Canada, who taught me that "Every human life is insignificant unless you, yourself make it great."

Grant D. Sylvester

Introduction

The good life is expensive. There is another way to live that doesn't cost as much but it isn't any good.
— Spanish distiller

For more than 25 years I have traveled to the corners of the globe, conducting personal-development seminars. More than half a million people have attended my seminars, looking for ways to improve the quality of their lives (which is very difficult to do without sufficient money). I have also studied many self-help books. Until now, we have not had a book that clearly explains, in a step-by-step fashion, how to accumulate wealth. You have such a guide in your hand. I strongly urge you to use it.

I have also worked with thousands of people employed by financial institutions. It wasn't long before I came to the shocking realization that very few of these people understood money. And even fewer had any. They were at a complete loss as to how to assist others in their accumulation of wealth.

Our society has become so engrossed with the idea of having a degree that we have almost completely neglected educating our students in the basic fundamentals of how to deal with a life of great wealth and unlimited service.

Grant Sylvester and his associates are different. They are part of a small, select group of individuals who truly understand money. He has used several basic fundamentals himself, and they work.

However, reading or memorizing this book will do you little or no good. You must study, think and understand its content; then, follow the paths that Grant Sylvester suggests; they will lead to the ultimate goal of wealth.

Grant's holistic approach to the accumulation of wealth is unique. He has done a masterful job of weaving together the psychological and practical changes we must make to enjoy the good life. He explains very clearly why money will not make you a better person but how it can provide you with the means to become a more effective one.

The good life costs a lot of money in today's fast-moving, materialistic world, but don't let that discourage you. You can most certainly enjoy the good life. When you understand and apply the tried-and-true principles Grant Sylvester shares with you, the changes in your financial world will amaze and delight you.

Wallace D. Wattles, who in 1903 wrote *The Science of Getting Rich,* once said, "If you want to do good, get rich first." Wattles was right. The good you can do if you have no money will be limited to what you can offer in person at any given time. However, when you have plenty of money, you are able to serve others in ways that extend far beyond one-on-one contact.

Regardless of your present financial position, you must understand that you can have money, all you want, but you must earn it. Before you settle into the first chapter, clearly understand that great wealth is something achieved by very few people. Most people live in ignorance of what you are about to learn, and they go through their entire lives barely earning enough money to get by.

If wealth is something that has escaped you up to this point in your life, you are not unusual. What is unusual is the fact that you are now doing something to correct your financial situation. I once heard that a definition of insanity was attempting to achieve better results in our lives without altering our behavior.

You must alter your behavior if you want to improve your financial situation. Grant Sylvester has clearly indicated many of the changes you must make. As you read you will see that these changes are not dramatic. On the contrary, they are quite simple. A few dollars properly invested every week will grow into a great fortune in time. But you must invest those few dollars and you must continue to invest them every week.

There is not only a need for the information in this book; there is a crying demand for it. As you begin to apply the principles in each chapter and your wealth begins to accumulate, remember the advice of Lord Bacon: "Money is a good servant but a bad master."

Bob Proctor
Author and Personal Development Consultant

Foreword

I come from a railroad family. My grandfathers and father had what they considered solid job security because they were able to "get on the railroad." In those days finding a job and holding it, no matter how backbreaking the work or how little the pay, was the goal of most people. The concept of financial planning was as remote to them as the Himalayas.

My sister and brothers and I were constantly urged to "get an education." My father used to tell us that "a person was worth a dollar an hour from the neck down, but had untold potential from the neck up." Get an education, join a large company and work steadily toward the top. At 65, take your pension and the gold watch and enjoy your retirement dinner. That was typical of the next generation and what passed for planning then.

Today we're told that young people will change jobs 10 times through their working lives and will shift careers 4 distinct times. Because of that, it's hard to develop much loyalty to a company. And with the advent of "downsizing," "outplacements," "early retirements," "severances" and "rationalization," today's employees know they cannot rely on the corporation for job security — they are going to have to depend on their own, flexible skills. Surveys tell us that 70% of baby-boomers would prefer to have their own businesses. Only 11% work because they like it; the other 89% work because they need the money.

Life has become a lot more complicated than it was 50 years ago. And the means society uses to part you from your hard-earned income are considerably more sophisticated. The pressures from outside and inside — our own psychological state — *not* to save or even to think about it systematically, are tremendous. Whether you are going to change jobs often on the way up, or you eventually quit to start your own business, a lot of well-thought-out financial planning will have to be part of your game-plan. To think otherwise is irresponsible. That means establishing financial goals as early as possible. With proper planning, and the miracle of time and compound interest, almost everybody can become financially independent to pursue a host of other options well before they reach middle age.

The approach of the current generation to careers may be considerably different from that of my generation, but some things haven't changed: it still takes a lot of old-fashioned perseverence, and patience, and perhaps a little bit of luck, to make those dreams come true. If you don't want to depend on luck, however, you will have to depend on financial planning. Financial planning for the average wage-earner is relatively new. Until recently such an esoteric concept was reserved for the wealthy who could afford high-priced professional advisors. Today the methods are simpler and the cost within reason for almost everybody. More than 90% of Canadians have the earning power to become financially self-reliant by middle or at least retirement age. All you need to do is add planning and perseverance to that earning power. But personal financial planning is not a simple mathematical exercise. Recognizing the human element and accommodating our human emotions in planning a secure financial future (and why most people don't do it) are what we're going to discuss in the following pages.

1

The Only Way to Financial Independence

I am a terrible money manager by nature. If I have money in my pocket, I spend it. If I have money in a readily accessible bank account, I take it out and buy things with it — not necessarily things I need, just things I want.

Perhaps I'm indiscreet to mention such a serious flaw in my character. After all, I have set myself up as an expert in personal financial planning. But I want to talk about my less-than-perfect personality (only so far as it pertains to managing my money, of course) for two special reasons.

Ironically, my very imperfections have led me to financial independence. When I am ready to leave the business world I will have enough money and more to support the comfortable kind of lifestyle my wife and I want to pursue. How that happened is something of a silk-purse-out-of-a-sow's-ear story. I realized some years ago that I was having a terrible time saving money, no matter what approach I tried, and I knew that I had better do something about it. With my own financial affairs I was like the chronic dieter: repeatedly falling on and off the food wagon and usually ending up heavier than ever before, though lighter in the wallet. When I realized this, it frightened me. At last I sat down to analyze my financial situation because I could not trust myself to control my spendthrift habits. I examined my years of experience in the business world first. The result was the first rough draft of the Money Jar system. I have refined the program constantly since, but what you read here is essentially what I designed to help myself, in spite of myself. The Money Jar system is a comprehensive personal financial-planning program designed to help me overcome the fact that I was my own worst financial enemy.

I'm not much different from most of you reading this book. We all indulge in a little financial misbehavior from time to time, and it's important that we realize and accept that fact. I've made my share of money-management mistakes over the years. This is completely normal. "To err is human, to forgive divine," wrote Alexander Pope. Forgive yourself your past financial follies and get on with the business of improving your money-management performance. The only reason to feel guilty about making money mistakes — and, in fact, you *should* lose a lot of sleep over it — is if you don't try to do something about your shortcomings.

Life is more complicated, more confusing and more challenging than ever before. We have more options, opportunities and choices than our parents and grandparents ever dreamed of. But we have more decisions to make as well, and a bewildering plethora of information, and misinformation, upon which to base those choices. Our society is one of the most affluent in the world. In many parts of the country, especially the urban areas, there is statistical full employment.

So you have the means to solve your financial problems if you choose to take the time and acquire the skill. The knowledge to develop and monitor a financial plan is freely available to all. The tax-based tools to help you to effectively follow a long-range plan are in place. Not to do so is inexcusable. If you don't plan for the future you are being irresponsible — toward yourself, toward the society that must support you later if you cannot do so yourself, and toward the family and dependents who rely on you.

And don't throw up your hands and say you can't do it because you're not a financial genius. If I could do it, you can too. By the time you have finished reading *The Money Jar,* you will have learned enough about personal financial planning to proceed confidently along the road to financial independence.

I should warn you: *The Money Jar* is not a get-rich-quick scheme. It is an effective program that will pay off for you if you have patience and if you stick to it. Follow its guidelines faithfully and, like the poet W.E. Henley, you'll eventually be able to say that, as far as your personal finances are concerned: "I am the master of my fate; I am the captain of my soul." In fact, you could be in the same position as Joe Pondosi of Vancouver Island who phoned me in Toronto a few years ago just to tell me that "we followed the [Money Jar] philosophy religiously and life has been very good to us. My career has prospered, the children are getting educated and we could, if we wanted to, retire today. It's a great feeling to be in our position, and I just want to thank you for giving us our start."

Financial Planning Is No Longer Just for the Privileged Few

At one time, personal financial planning was the prerogative of the wealthy who could afford a phalanx of high-priced tax and investment advisors. But the financial-planning industry has grown tremendously in the 1970s and 1980s. There is dependable professional advice available in almost every urban center. In many cases professionals' services will cost you nothing because their compensation comes from commission on various financial products you might put into your plan. If you do choose a planner who uses a fee structure, you can minimize the cost by doing much of the work yourself, then bringing in the planner for the last-minute touches needed to complete an effective plan.

I have dealt with thousands of clients, clients of all income levels. I have witnessed their mistakes and seen the results of their misguided judgment. In some cases I have contributed to their successes. The Money Jar philosophy is not just a fad, in vogue today but tomorrow supplanted by another financial fashion. It is solid, prudent financial practice, based on my 35-year extensive background in the financial industry.

For some years now I have concentrated on developing my practice as a professional financial planner. I felt the need for personal financial planning was so great, especially among those with incomes in the $25,000 to $80,000 range, that I started my own company. I am now president of Money Concepts Canada Inc., a personal financial-planning franchise organization with more than 70 outlets in Canada. The company specializes in using the Money Jar system to help people with average incomes plan for a better financial future.

Before this I served a number of years as senior marketing vice-president of a major insurance company. I have been chairman of the board of the Life Insurance Marketing and Research Association of Hartford, Connecticut. My educational credentials include a Bachelor of Arts, an RHU (Registered Health Underwriter), a CLU (Chartered Life Underwriter), a CFP (Chartered Financial Planner) and an RFP (Registered Financial Planner).

Today I speak to groups as diverse as the Welding Supply Dealers of Canada and the Canadian Life and Health Insurance Association; from the Shriners in Barrie, Ontario, to the Insight Forum. I have made numerous appearances on radio and television, from Newfoundland to British Columbia.

The Money Jar system of personal financial planning has been described in *The Financial Post,* the *Financial Times, Canadian Business* and *Small Business* magazines and in many other daily and weekly newspapers throughout Canada. CBC TV's "Marketplace" has rated it as the top service of its kind. Many of our franchise presidents across the country lecture on personal financial planning in their local universities or community colleges.

IBM, the computer giant, once demonstrated our company's software (used as part of the planning process) at a financial-services conference. Afterward they wrote: "The degree of interest can only be described by the large number of questions . . . [including] where can we buy it?"

The Story of 100 Men

I like to start off my seminars with what I call "The Story of 100 Men." Like the equivalent story of 100 women, it effectively illustrates the financial position that most of us are in.

Let's look at the history of 100 men at the start of their careers and again at the end, assuming they all retire at age 65. Between the time those 100 men began their careers (from age 18 or 21 or so), and the time they retired, each earned more than $1 million on average. Those with specialized skills or a university education might have taken in more — perhaps in excess of $1.5 million.

Each of those who started out together had different personal goals and interests. But they all had one thing in common: they expected to be successful. Yet strange things happen on the way to retirement. At age 65

1 will be rich;
8 will be well-to-do;
24 will have died;
14 will still have to work;
53 will be dependent or destitute.

So, by age 65, about 91 men out of 100 are either dead or almost dead-broke. The statistics for women are even more depressing: respectively 1 rich, 2 well-to-do, 4 dead, 11 still having to work and 82 dependent or destitute. That makes 97% dead or dead-broke.

Statistics Canada tells us that among individuals over the age of 65,

> 11.0% have annual incomes of less than $5,000;
> 61.7% have annual incomes of less than $10,000; and
> 79.8% have annual incomes of less than $15,000.

The median income of all Canadians aged 65 is $8,525 (males $10,762 and females $7,542).

All of these statistics are real, in a wealthy country where we "enjoy" one of the highest living standards in the world. In the past 50 years too, we have watched Canada's uninterrupted economic expansion.

Given our general affluence, the favorable (yes, that's right — favorable) tax laws, and the amount of financial information available, there is absolutely no reason for anybody reading this book to be in the bottom two categories of the 100-men story. If you understand the principles and apply the techniques outlined in *The Money Jar* you can shift your position on that list from one of the 65 victims to, if not rich, at least not destitute. You could be financially independent.

This assumes, of course, that you consider eventual financial independence "a consummation devoutly to be wish'd." Financial independence means different things to different people. For some it could mean saving enough money to finance a return to school or university at age 45. Others might eventually want to flee the rat-race with enough savings to finance the start-up of their own, more satisfying businesses. Financial autonomy might well mean simply a comfortable income in retirement, or an early retirement.

Whatever your various motivations for accumulating capital, you undoubtedly have a particular goal in mind or at least some kind of wish list. Why, then, are so many of us financially unprepared when it comes time to undertake the big change we've wanted to make for so long? How do the 95% of us account for the fact that, in addition to not being wealthy, we can't adequately maintain ourselves financially in later life? Something is dreadfully wrong here. After all, we didn't plan to fail financially. Perhaps, though, we *did* fail to make plans.

Planning is what makes the difference between financial comfort or financial dependency in later life. But only 9 Canadian men and women out of every 100 seem to be aware that a systematic personal financial plan, plus plenty of patience, are the keys to ultimate financial independence. Even with the most elaborate plan you can't become financially autonomous overnight. Only by following the basic guidelines of a plan over many years and giving it adequate time will its full potential develop. You can't force a fine wine to mature faster than its nature will allow; and you can't force the maturation of a financial plan. As the international financier Bernard M. Baruch once put it: "The success or failure of a long range savings and investment plan is not predicated on the rate of return. Its success depends on the use of a systematic plan of putting money in and leaving it there."

That's not always easy. I remember one instance (and there have been more than one) when my own impatience has got the better of me. Back in the 1950s one of my aunts came to visit our family. She had been touring and her travels had taken her to Ottawa and a visit to the Royal Canadian Mint. To commemorate her visit to us she brought a few presents. Mine was a gleaming set of freshly minted coins neatly mounted in a cardboard folder: a brand-new silver dollar, a 50-cent piece, a 25-cent piece, a 10-cent piece, a nickel and a penny. I was ecstatic to have such a souvenir and was determined to make it the beginning of a large collection. But a couple of years later, when I was almost flat broke, I wanted to take a special friend out to dinner. So, I bought our meal with my aunt's gift (it was a modest dinner), regretting at the time only that I had parted with a rather attractive souvenir. Not long ago I was in a coin-collectors' shop in Toronto and noticed several coin sets on display. Out of mild curiosity I checked the current value of the 1954 set. It floored me. The set I traded for dinner so many years ago currently was selling for $540. Isn't hindsight wonderful? We usually regret the mistakes we made in the past; yet we're still making mistakes today about the future. One of the benefits of personal financial planning is that it helps us avoid repeating our mistakes.

The Mathematics of Planned Savings Are in Your Favor

Many of the middle- and even low-income clients who pass through my office figure it's hardly worth trying to save any money because they believe that they have to earn a huge amount during their lifetimes before they can become financially independent. That's not true, of course. But this attitude is typical of the many myths and misconceptions about money that often inhibit peoples' saving programs. You do not have to be part of the high–tax-bracket crowd to end up with a fistful of money when you retire. If, for instance, you start saving a modest $20 a week at age 30, by the time you are 65 your registered retirement savings plan (RRSP) would contain a handsome $333,485 (assuming you earn 10% interest on it). If you were to earn 11% interest on your savings (and that is well within reason), that additional 1% would add another $100,472 to your already substantial nestegg. A reward of $433,957 is worth summoning up the mild discipline required to save $20 a week, isn't it?

If you are one of those fortunate enough to be earning nearly $40,000 a year by the time you are 30, and you expect to maintain or increase that level throughout your working life, you can generate an astoundingly large pool of capital that will eventually set you free from any financial worry. Consider the high side of RRSP saving: if your annual income is enough to allow the maximum $7,500 RRSP contribution (as of year-end 1989) each year, for 35 years, from age 30 on, you would retire with a whopping $2,235,951 (assuming interest at 10%). Or a meagre $811,363 if you wanted to escape the rat-race at 55 and go do your own thing.

But saving $20 a week, or $7,500 each year, is only a single step in the process of creating a comprehensive personal financial plan. A financial plan helps you chart a safe course for your lifetime voyage. But, if you haven't taken adequate precautions, any voyage can be abruptly swamped by unexpected financial storms. The operative word here is *comprehensive.* A comprehensive financial plan is not simply an RRSP. Or a savings account. Or a stock you bought with last year's bonus. A financial plan is a long-term, strategic scheme that takes into consideration every possible major financial need throughout your lifetime. It includes objectives, procedures, stages and techniques, every one of them related to your particular circumstances and your particular aspirations for financial independence.

In the most simplified terms a financial plan is a dispassionate and accurate assessment of where your finances are today, a thoughtful projection of where you want them to be when you reach your goals, and a series of individual action plans, designed for your personal situation, that will enable you to achieve those goals within the time period you specify.

There Is More to Planning Than Money

One major by-product of financial planning is peace of mind. Once you have developed a financial plan, you have a firm structure to lean on and specific objectives to follow. The steadfast shelter offered by that structure adds a measure of stability to your life. It relieves you of a constant anxiety that lurks in the back of every person's mind as the years go on: "I really should do something to secure my future." Following a plan means you don't have to agonize over ad hoc decisions every time some new money problem, or opportunity, arises. You are relieved of "the torment of choice," as novelist Saul Bellow refers to it, because your various action plans virtually make the decisions for you. You can be reasonably certain financial catastrophe won't overwhelm you because your plan anticipates the worst and prepares for it. You can quickly assess unforeseen but interesting financial opportunities that present themselves, and if they don't fit in with your plan's objectives, you can resolutely pass them up without wasting time wondering whether you made a mistake. Remember, a bargain isn't a bargain if you can't afford it or if you end up with a costly white elephant. A financial plan helps you avoid being trampled by the white elephants that eager brokers and considerate friends with "inside information" often put in your path. Peace of mind is priceless and should be thought of as one of the essential reasons for planning.

Another benefit of planning: the amazing amount of time you will save if you really follow the course your plan has charted. Because you already have established your goal and set out your criteria for reaching it, you don't have to repeatedly decide what to do, how to do it, in what way, with how much and when. Your mind will be free of the kind of anxiety that those without plans continually wrestle with. And you'll have more time to spend doing things you enjoy.

Why Does the Money Jar Approach Work?

There are dozens of books on the market about personal finances. Some of them are about money management in general. Some touch on only certain aspects of planning. Most of them are about investing and often tell you more than you want to know about the options or the gold markets. These are how-to books. Most of them are intended for readers who have money and want to know how to invest it or how to minimize their taxes on it — information that often becomes obsolete very quickly because of changing tax laws and industry regulations.

The Money Jar differs from these books in three essential ways:

1) *The Money Jar* approach is only about planning and is simple. It is consistent, comprehensive but easy to understand and easy to carry out. It does not tell you more than you need to know.
2) *The Money Jar* approach answers the question: Why? It is not simply a how-to book. It is based on understanding — understanding the problems we have so it is easier to deal with them. The psychological barriers to building a comfortable financial future are just as important as our lack of knowledge of the specific planning process.
3) *The Money Jar* accentuates the positive. It doesn't dwell on the immense difficulties of acquiring a huge fortune, or completing complex, sophisticated plans you seldom understand. It does not endorse the concept of pasting pictures of fat people on the refrigerator door to frighten away the chronic nibbler.

Number 3 — being positive — may seem obvious. But in the past few years there has been a huge growth in the application of positive reinforcement to human endeavor, with the most positive results. A few years ago I heard a former army officer describe his months in an enemy prison camp, often in solitary confinement. "The only way I kept sane," he said, "was to play, over and over, one by one, stroke by stroke, the 18 holes of my favorite golf club back home. I imagined every nuance of playing, from the type of ball I was using, to my grip on the club, to the shifting of my weight when I swung. Even the feel of the grass under my feet.

"Needless to say, I played every shot perfectly and usually broke par. This was quite satisfying to me because in real life I usually shot around 100 for 18 holes."

The officer eventually was released and returned home. One of the first things he did was get his clubs out and go to play that golf course he had mastered so often in his prison-camp imagination. On his first round, the 100-stroke golfer scored a one-under-par 71. The power of positive reinforcement is immense.

So how is the Money Jar system structured — how does it work? What do you have to know to set up a successful personal financial plan? What are the elements that go into a plan? Well, first you have to become aware of the dark forces within yourself, every one of them nurtured by inherited myths and misinformation about money management. These internal forces hold you back from achieving your goal of financial independence. You must also be able to recognize the forces from without, those generated by the society you live in, that repeatedly erect roadblocks in your path to successful saving and planning programs. Then finally you must learn the mechanics of putting a plan together — the kind of information you need to put together yourself, and the kind you might need a personal financial planner to provide for you.

In my seminars I sometimes characterize this three-stage approach as a recipe for financial success. If you want your financial plan to succeed, as you would with your favorite recipe, you can't leave any essential ingredient out. So in the next chapter let's quickly run through the list of a plan's essential ingredients. After that we'll examine each in more detail and you'll learn how they blend together effectively to help you achieve your goal of financial independence.

2

Ingredients in the Money Jar Recipe

Not everybody, of course, needs a personal financial plan. If you have inherited more money than you know what do do with or you have recently won the lottery or you are chief executive officer of a major corporation, with a huge salary, you may not need to plan much beyond a basic strategy to help you hold on to your money through good and bad times. Perhaps you have immense willpower and can save substantial sums every year, and are a whiz in the stock market. In such circumstances you may not need a comprehensive financial plan.

But the rest of us need a little help if we want to become financially independent.

When you are 20 years old it's sometimes hard to understand why you should be saving money when you'd rather be spending it on pizza and a couple of new compact disks. So most of us tend to postpone seriously starting to save for the long term until it is more "convenient." But it is almost never convenient. If it isn't one thing you want to buy, it's another. It's only human to put off today saving for tomorrow. But procrastination is the thief of financial freedom.

If you have put off saving until middle age or weren't in a position to save any earlier, all is not lost. There are many things you can do to make up for lost time. We'll talk about some of them in Chapter 17.

Before you can construct a financial plan, you require background information and raw materials. Information is the mortar that holds the planning bricks together. You also need a good understanding of human nature — especially your own — because that nature so often conspires against you when you want to implement and follow your plan but can't quite manage to do so consistently.

Every strategic plan — and a personal financial plan is just that — consists of various elements, or mini-plans, that are independent of one another and can be carried out separately. But they all fit and work together, like a jigsaw puzzle, to complete the main plan.

The First and Second Secrets of Financial Success

There are two simple rules, or secrets, that underlie the successful design and implementation of a personal financial plan. They are easy to understand and we'll consider them in chapters 3 and 4.

Runaway Emotions Destroy Your Best Money-Management Intentions

Suddenly abandoning a carefully drawn-up personal budget (like dropping out of a crash diet after a few deprived days) is a typical example of letting emotions overrule financial prudence. You go on a spending spree to compensate for a bitter dispute with your spouse, wiping out not only your savings but your good intentions. Every time you go on an emotional binge you weaken your ability to stick to the next budget you develop.

We all have an emotional side to our personalities. But when it comes to money management, you can't allow your emotions to wreck your financial plan. You must understand how your misplaced emotional reactions can sabotage a financially secure future. That understanding can lead to the development of mechanisms that help you act, if not think, more rationally when it comes to money management. Your financial plan must have a temperate emotional climate in which to grow at its natural pace and come to a full and profitable maturity.

We Don't Save the Right Way, or For the Right Reasons

Compared to people in other countries, Canadians are pretty good savers although most don't do it in a systematic way. In the difficult economic times of the early 1980s, we saved almost 18% of our disposable income (income left after paying taxes and basic necessities). That figure has declined as economic times have improved but we are still squirreling away more than the mere 3% to 7% we did in the 1950s and 60s.

The trouble is when most of us start saving, we generally go about it in the wrong way and for the wrong reasons. That's because we don't understand proper savings goals. We tend to bundle all our reserves into one big grab bag called "savings" despite the different purposes we might have in mind for the money later. Whenever we want to buy a house, a washing machine or a new car, or take a trip to Hawaii, we grab what we need from our one savings bag. Only too often the bag is empty by the time we need to educate the children, fund our retirement, drop out of the rat-race to start our own business or go sketching in Greenland for a year.

Everybody Out There Is Trying to Separate You from Your Money

But the battle for financial independence is not as simple as merely controlling your emotions. You are also surrounded by armies of marketing experts whose primary purpose is to breech the walls of your strongest resolve and to annihilate your efforts to restrict overspending. Having a personal financial plan helps you to learn to close your ears (and eyes) to the lure of the marketeers' siren songs so your hopes for financial autonomy don't founder on waves of impulsive spending.

The Key to Saving

Saving is one thing. What you do with your growing bundle of assets is quite another. On the one hand you must protect the assets you have. On the other, you must stimulate them to grow at a rate faster than inflation, so you'll be able to live off the income they generate later in life. We'll look into some ways of doing that, and survey the merits of various types of investments.

We'll also discuss the misunderstandings that thwart the well-meaning attempts of many of us to save effectively. And I'll suggest a few techniques that might help, as they have helped me.

RRSPs: The Most Accessible (and Misunderstood) Method of Saving

A registered retirement savings plan (RRSP) is perhaps the most useful, and misused, way of handling your savings. An RRSP usually is an essential ingredient in the recipe for financial freedom and so you must be perfectly clear how they work and what they are for. I have included a primer in *The Money Jar* — not an exhaustive dissertation — on the proper use of RRSPs.

Working 9 to 5 Is Not What It Used to Be

The nature of work in our society has changed radically since the days of our parents and grandparents. Life was more secure psychologically, and sometimes economically. Social and economic change was a good deal slower than today. If you had a good job with a large and benevolent firm, you could usually look forward to comfortable if sometimes modest retirement with the help of company and government pensions, even if you couldn't expect complete financial independence. In many cases homes were larger and could accommodate older family members who could not take care of themselves.

But not today. The cost of living and our greater material expectations make it more difficult for the working generation to support less fortunate and older relatives. You can't count on a lengthy career and financial security with one company. Government allowances alone are too little to live on and if you happen to have a company pension plan, you will likely find the retirement income you receive from it is not as much as you expected.

The fact is you cannot count on anybody or anything else to provide for your financial future. The only way to do that is to create and follow a financial plan of your own — the odds of succeeding that way are infinitely greater than depending on the lottery.

The Insidious Cost of Living

Another piece you'll have to fit into your financial plan jigsaw is the effect of inflation. Inflation is not just a buzzword that economists, business writers and politicians love to use. Like death and taxes, it is real, always with us and insidious. How often have you thought that it doesn't matter too much if inflation pushes up food costs because you'll compensate for that by piling up a lot more interest in your savings accounts? Anyway, you'll probably get a cost-of-living raise from your employer, right?

Wrong. Unfortunately, you can never catch up that way. Inflation is 4%, so you get a 4% raise. "Terrific," you think, "automatic catch-up." Think again. You'll pay from 30% to 50% of that raise to the government in the form of taxes. So, you'll still be behind. Inflation inexorably eats away much of what you have or hope to have, especially when you are on a fixed income after retiring. You have to consider the effect of inflation when you draw up your financial plan. If you do, you can minimize its worst effects.

Government: A Hand in Every Pocket

Like it or not, every one of us has partners in Ottawa, our province and our municipality. Forget that at your peril when it comes to financial planning. As recently as 20 years ago, governments were our junior partners and took a mere one-third of our earnings to pay for the various services and programs they contend Canadians demand. The Fraser Institute has determined that the average Canadian now works from New Year's Eve until early July solely to pay for all forms of taxes in Canada. Today governments have become the senior partners in this equation and we have become the juniors.

So, you have to design your financial plans to minimize taxes, especially since governments appear to have an increasingly insatiable appetite for more and more of your money. Not everybody can be a tax expert, but you can call upon experts to advise you. A professional financial planner or an accountant can supply the tax information you need. Professional assistance is a must when you reach a certain stage in financial planning.

Protecting Those You Leave...

You can tap into the best tax expertise available and design the most systematic and effective savings program, but if your premature death wipes out your dependents' source of income, all that effort is wasted. A breadwinner must insure his or her life adequately so that death is not financially catastrophic for the survivors. And life insurance is just as important for single people too. It is another integral part of your financial plan.

Life insurance is actually for the living. Most of the money paid out by insurance companies is to help people augment their retirement income, or it is a loan against the cash value of a policy to help a policyholder through a temporary financial pinch, or it is a savings plan designed eventually to lead to financial self-reliance.

Canadians are among the most insured people in the world, but our total insurance coverage represents only 1.5 times the national income. Applied on an individual basis, total coverage of 1.5 times your yearly income is not nearly enough to maintain your beneficiaries in the lifestyle they probably have become accustomed to (if your coverage matches the national average). To assure adequate life coverage, you must buy the right coverage for the right reason. So, you have to be aware of the types of insurance coverages available, what the newest insurance wrinkles are, what policy limitations exist and what the specific benefits are. Once you know that, you won't be at the mercy of an insurance sales agent who might not be as objective as he or she should be. After all, you must be the one to make the final decision what is best for your circumstances, not a third party.

. . . And Yourself

Imagine a sudden, hideous car accident, or even a wrenching tumble on a ski slope. In a matter of seconds you are completely paralyzed. You can't work for three years or perhaps the rest of your life. With no money coming in, any emergency savings fund you have can be quickly exhausted.

Don't think this couldn't happen to you. In fact, the chances that it will happen are considerably greater than you would imagine. Even if you develop an emergency fund by putting aside as much as 10% of your income every year, you could still be in trouble: a lengthy disability can easily wipe out a lifetime of savings.

You can, however, protect yourself against such an eventuality by purchasing disability insurance. This form of insurance is not widely understood but it is just as important as life insurance in your financial plan.

Putting It All Together

By now you will have grasped that a personal financial plan is more than putting away a few dollars every month. Accumulating all the data, then putting it together in a comprehensive financial plan is not the easiest thing to do, but it can be exceptionally rewarding. Planning is a 6-step process, and we'll examine each of those steps in some detail. This will help prepare you should you want to develop a financial plan yourself. And it will show you what to expect if you choose to use a professional financial planner to do the job.

Speaking of choosing, your choice of an outside planning expert is critical. We'll look at some of the criteria you should apply when making that choice.

Perhaps by now you are thinking that almost everything I have outlined so far in this chapter is addressed only to young people; and that the only way that you could ever be free of financial worry is if your parents started saving Family Allowance checks in your name as soon as you were born, and later on you kept saving at the same or a greater rate. Getting an early start and keeping it up for a long period is essential to maximize savings. But don't despair if you haven't been able to.

Perhaps you've suddenly become widowed or divorced in your 40s or 50s and have little in the way of assets. Perhaps you thought the government or company pension plan would support you well enough, but you find they don't. It's true, if you start late you might never soar to the same savings heights as the early birds, but there are alternatives you can follow to help you get off the ground and you shouldn't have to worry where your next meal will come from when you finally do retire. We'll explore some of these alternatives in the last chapter.

In the appendix at the end of the book you will find reproduced some pertinent sections from an actual financial plan.

By the time you finish *The Money Jar* you should have a pretty good idea of most of the impediments that tend to deflect you from your planned path to financial independence, and how to get around them and back on track toward realizing your financial goals.

3

The First Secret of Financial Freedom

Not long ago I was at Pearson International Airport near Toronto starting the first leg of a business trip to the United States. As I boarded the plane I spotted an old friend who was taking the same flight, so we decided to sit together.

Dave is an industrial psychologist but has a keen interest in the state and future of the somewhat turbulent financial-services industry in Canada. He has been wondering, like many others, which of the firms now jockeying for position in the partially deregulated financial sector are likely to emerge the winners, and how they are going to do it. He knew I had given a few talks on the subject and had written some articles about it, so we chatted.

We covered a lot of ground, from the power of advertising, the concentration of distribution systems, and the ability to develop products and services the public needs and accepts as at least partial solutions to their financial problems. He was delighted when he found my views coincided with his. I guess he is much like I am (and a lot of others, I think) when often we ask people's advice not so much in the expectation of learning anything, but rather to reaffirm our own views and opinions.

As the "buckle your seat belt" sign flashed off and we leveled out, heading south, he asked me a key question: "Grant, in spite of all these factors we've talked about — marketing, capital distribution systems, manufacturing capabilities, ingenuity and the rest — what in your opinion is the single most important ingredient for the eventual success of a business organization?"

I had been through a lot of corporate-planning exercises, so I was ready for that one. "Find out what people want and then give it to them."

He nodded and said that he generally knew what his clients wanted of him, but "when it comes to financial services, what do people really want? What do your clients want?"

"That's easy," I said. "They want financial independence."

"Well, then, how are you going to give it to them?"

"Dave," I said, "I can't give clients financial independence. But I can show them how to achieve it, and I can help them realize that it is not all that difficult to do."

"Then how about summing up the secret of financial independence in 50 words or less?"

"I don't know about 50 words, but there are actually two secrets, and both of them are surprisingly simple. The first one, which goes back to ancient Babylonian days, is: *You pay yourself first — and I mean first — before you pay anything to anyone else, including your rent and your taxes.*"

The usual practice for most of us, Dave agreed, is to pay all our bills when we get our paychecks. We expect to save at least some of what is left. But unfortunately there's seldom anything left, so saving is out the window. So the first thing you do when you get your take-home pay is to write a check to yourself, for as much as 10% of it, if you can afford to. Then pay your bills. If you have anything left, you can go out on the town and spend it without feeling guilty. Paying yourself first is probably the single most important thing you can do to achieve financial independence.

Fred Smith, the owner of one of our Money Concepts Financial Centres in Saskatchewan, emphasized this concept rather well, I thought, in a seminar he was presenting. He pointed out to the group that, according to a 1989 report on the nation prepared by *The Financial Post,* average personal income in 1988 was estimated at $40,357 per employee. Average after-tax income was $31,322. That means most of the difference, about $9,000, was deducted at source by employers on behalf of Revenue Canada.

Fred asked the group how many of them, if they had to write that check for the total $9,000 to Revenue Canada on April 30, 1989, would have been able to. Not many said yes.

Whatever you might think of it, the government isn't stupid when it comes to siphoning money from your pocket to its. It realized as long ago as 1943 that the only way it was going to get all its taxes from the taxpayer was *to make sure it, the government, was paid first.* So it passed legislation that forced employers to deduct tax from each paycheck, in advance, before the taxpayers got their hot hands on it.

The government wasn't, and still isn't, taking any chances. Nor should you. Pay yourself first, preferably before you see a penny. Here are a few ways you can do it:

1) Open a savings-only account at your bank or trust company. Have a fixed amount transferred automatically each month from your checking to the savings account. If you don't have much in your checking account, you aren't likely to spend much.
2) Make a similar arrangement with your company's payroll department. Perhaps it has an arrangement that lets you buy Canada Savings Bonds this way. CSBs won't give you the highest return, but establishing the discipline of regular savings is almost more important.
3) See if your company will set up a group RRSP for employees. Then make regular, automatic contributions to it through payroll deduction. This approach has the added benefit of reducing your tax burden.
4) Buy some whole life or universal life insurance. Make arrangements with the insurance company to take automatic deductions from your bank checking account for the premiums.
5) You can make similar arrangements to buy mutual funds with automatic deductions from your bank account. You can invest as little as $50 a month with most funds. If you buy a front-end-load fund (sales commissions taken out of your payments) make sure the commission is taken a bit from each deposit, not all at once or even over a couple of years.

As the flight attendant slipped our lunch trays in front of us, Dave shook his head, a bit bemused. "Grant," he said, "I can hardly wait to get home and tell my kids about this. I want them to get started becoming financially independent right away.

"Your idea is so simple I can't believe I didn't think it out myself. But I didn't. How in heaven's name did you come up with such an approach?"

"I was just lucky, I guess," I said. "When I graduated from university at 21 I was forced to save because I was the wage-earner in the family. I also knew the value of and the need for life insurance because my father died when I was 17 and he left relatively little insurance.

"So, that's where I started. Every six months when I got a raise I bought another policy. At the end of two years I had four life insurance policies, each of them with savings components. In those days, life insurance was one of the best ways of investing. It still is, if you know what to buy and from whom.

"Then I changed jobs and the personnel manager at my new company said to me, 'Grant, if you put away 5% of your income we will match that 5% and tuck the whole 10% away into a savings fund that will be available for you in later years.'

"I didn't embrace the idea with a great deal of relish. I figured setting aside 5% of my income was a tough chore. But they didn't give me a choice — that pension plan was included in the terms of my employment. That started when I was 23. Later on the company made the arrangement even more attractive to maximize my contribution into that plan. And so did the income tax department.

"Dave, I am still 7 or 8 years from retirement, and of course I am no longer with that company. But that pension will be mine when I turn 65. Do you know that my portion of just the increase in value of that retirement fund from month to month right now is greater than my current gross salary each month?

"And by the time I am 65, the monthly increase in the value of those assets and interest will probably be twice what I earn every month. I feel kind of comforted by that. It's a substantial pension to look forward to."

4

The Second Secret of Financial Freedom

"What about the second secret for financial success?" Dave asked.

"It's equally simple," I replied.

"*Start early. Do it now, and don't wait until even a few months from now.*"

I could see that my answer was so simple and unsophisticated that Dave needed a little clarification. So I told him the story of Helen and Jack, a young couple who graduated together from university and married right away at the age of 22. They both went out to work and became a two-income family. They planned to start their family in about 6 years so Helen, realizing she might have a short working life, opened an RRSP and began saving money right from her first paycheck. She wasn't earning a lot, but she put by $200 a month for a $2,400 yearly contribution. In the meantime Jack was saving for a downpayment on a house and was making car payments, as his share.

Sure enough, 6 years later, when Helen was 28, she announced she was pregnant, and stopped working. She also stopped making any more RRSP contributions, since she needed money for the baby and to help furnish the house they would soon move into.

By this time Jack had saved the downpayment they needed for the house and had been promoted three times. He felt he must now look to the future, especially with a baby on the way, so he opened an RRSP for the first time. He realized he had a little catching up to do. He would make the same RRSP $2,400-per-year contribution that Helen used to, but planned to continue doing so until he was at the traditional retirement age of 65 — in other words, for the following 37 years.

Dave was starting to fidget as I went on about Helen and Jack. He probably thought he could see what was coming, and the whole scenario was a bit simplistic for him. So I summed up quickly.

"Dave, assume the couple was reasonably astute and they both earned the same rate of interest — averaging 12% a year during the time they saved. Helen had put $2,400 a year into her RRSP for the six years she worked outside the home. That amounted to a total contribution of $14,400. Jack, who started 6 years later, had also contributed $2,400 a year, but for 37 years. His total input was $88,800.

"The question is, my friend, which spouse had the greater amount of RRSP money at age 65?"

Dave quickly came back with the obvious answer: it must be Jack, since he had been saving for 37 years. When he noticed the smirk on my face he added, "Grant, don't tell me that Helen, who had saved for only 6 years, had the greater amount?"

"You're wrong on both counts. They had almost identical amounts in their RRSPs on their 65th birthdays — grand totals of close to $1,700,000 each." (Actually Helen had almost $100,000 more — not much difference considering the total amount.) (See Figure 1.)

Helen — Saves $200 per Month for 6 years
— Stops Deposits —
Accumulates to Age 65 at 12%

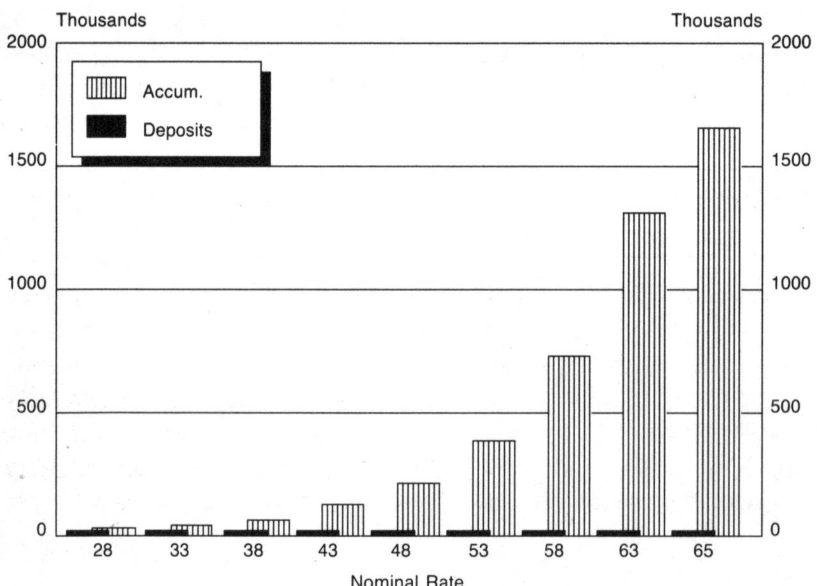

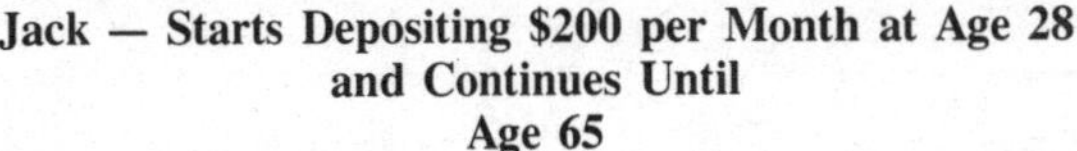

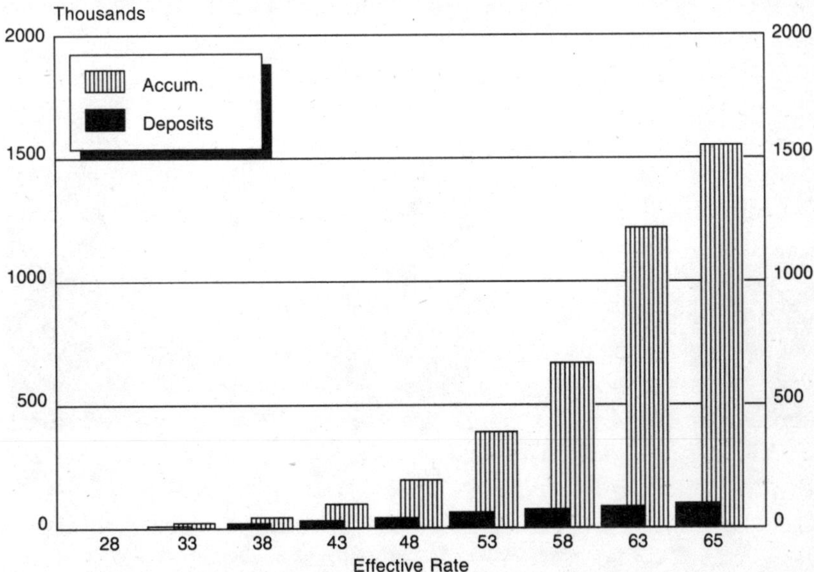

Figure 1: Most people would agree that starting to save early in a RRSP ($200 a month for six years — a total of $14,400) might be easier than starting six years later and saving the same amount per month for 37 years (a total of $18,800). The result at age 65 is almost the same: about $1,700,000. It pays to be an early starter.

Obviously, salting away a modest amount for a short period early in life is the most effective way to ensure financial independence. Time and the compounding of interest are working for you. They work whether your savings are sheltered from tax or not. But the growth is more dramatic inside a tax shelter.

I furnished Dave with a further example of how much it can cost to delay saving even for one year. The Templeton Growth Fund, one of the world's largest and oldest mutual funds, has kept track of investments since 1954. The fund's records show that if you had invested $100 a month for the previous 16 years you would have a nest-egg of $102,244 by 1989. If you had waited just one more year to start investing, you would only have $86,778 in 1989. That one-year delay in saving $1,200 would have cost you $15,456. (See Figure 2.)

THE HIGH COST OF WAITING TO SAVE

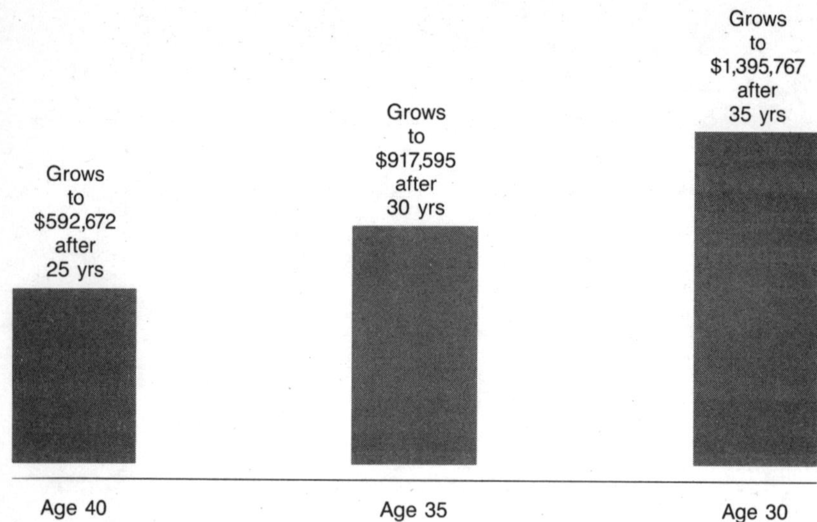

Figure 2: Assume a deposit (in an RRSP) of $7,500 per year earning 8% a year interest. If you wait 5 years to start, you will have a "waiting cost" of $440,622. If you wait 10 years, it will "cost" you $828,095.

To make the same point even more graphically, I told Dave that (in today's dollars) if he were 35 years old and started putting away the maximum permissible RRSP investment every year ($7,500 for the 1988 tax year), he would be able to retire with an income of $5,000 per month at age 60. But if he waited until he was age 40 to start saving the same amount — just five years later — his retirement income at age 60 would be exactly half, only $2,500 monthly. Even if he doubled his contributions for the last 20 years, he still couldn't catch up.

Cutting Back Won't Hurt, Even a Little

For much of the rest of the flight Dave and I discussed the psychological inhibitions that seem to prevent people from learning the simple lesson of saving from an early age. After all, it is not a new idea or a difficult one to comprehend. As a psychologist, Dave was able to talk about this aspect more authoritatively than I. It boils down to the fact, he concluded, that most of us are deathly afraid that saving today will reduce our standard of living. That fear is groundless. But if we think about it dispassionately, most of us would have to admit that, as work does, according to Parkinson's Law ("Work expands to fill the time available for its completion"), our spending expands to the extent of the money made available for it. And some of us spend even more than we make available to ourselves.

The truth of the matter is that if we did cut back on our spending by a modest amount we would still get by admirably. Our basic standard of living would not be affected because the amount we squeezed back, and saved, would come from those dollars that we spend needlessly, often foolishly every month. When Chrysler automobile workers' pay was cut back by 10% one year, the result was very few mortgage foreclosures and no suicides on record. We all can cut back our spending and save a little. All we need is the incentive and a little self-discipline.

Why Is It Never Convenient to Start Saving?

Every one of you reading these words (and I am no exception) could provide a list as long as your arm why you can't cut back and start saving the minute you put down this book. If it is January, obviously you can't start now because you are still paying off the Christmas bills. February is just as bad because you are still getting over Christmas bills and trying to put a little aside for theater tickets and a couple of dinners out. You'd really like to join friends for a week's skiing at Whistler or the Laurentians. By March you are feeling the full effects of winter's expenses: heating costs, a new winter coat, winter tires for the car, etc. In April it is out of the question because you've got to pay the balance of income tax due. May and June are inconvenient because you have to spend a fair amount on annuals and fertilizer for the garden or spruce up your home with a paint job and get ready for summer vacation. In July and August you are spending everything you have on a well-earned vacation. Vacations are over by September but the kids are back in school and university and they need new clothes, textbooks, travel and tuition fees. October is a bad month for saving. You may be helping the children with travel costs when they come home for Thanksgiving or replacing aging living room furniture. In November you start the Christmas-shopping process, and naturally it's out of the question to cut back in December because of the extra costs of the festive season. In fact, December often eats up not only any surplus you have laboriously built up but frequently dumps you into a financial pit from which you have to start climbing in January. The cycle repeats itself each year, and each year you're becoming more entrenched.

So what's the answer? There is never a convenient time to start saving, so the only time is right now. You have to start saving today, systematically and with regularity. There will never be a time in life when it is easier. You know the story: when you are young, you're enjoying yourself, you are trying to make up for the bare (financial) subsistence of school days. You want to buy a car, do some traveling — all those things that are important to do before you settle down and get married. Ask a 20-year-old if it's a convenient time to save. Nine-and-a-half times out of ten you'll get the answer: "Certainly not. The idea is ridiculous."

A 30-year-old will tell you that the cost of establishing a home, perhaps marrying and starting to raise a family, precludes any type of savings. A 40-year-old will advise you that the cost of education or moving to a larger home is so overwhelming that it's an impossible time to save. Most 50-year-olds will agree that it's getting too late for serious saving and they wish they had started in their 20s or 30s. To start in your 50s you have to think in terms of saving 20% to 40% of your income if you want a reasonable retirement standard of living. And that's *really* tough.

Being an Early Bird Reduces Risk

There's another good reason to start saving early: if you do, you don't have to be the best investor in the world. Even the most conservative investments, if you add to them systematically, will pay off handsomely over a long period of time. Many of the better-performing mutual funds have rates of return well in excess of 15%, and some in excess of 20% over 10 years or more. But even if you invest cautiously and are satisfied with a return of, say, 12%, you can become financially independent in a relatively short period of time. If you start early enough.

The "fasten your seat belts" sign started flashing as we started our descent and I mentioned to Dave that I was writing *The Money Jar.*

"If even a few readers become convinced that the secret to financial independence is not so secret," I said, "and the book helps start them on the right foot, then all the hours I have put into it will have been well spent."

5

Money Management: An Emotional Experience

Money management is usually not just a mathematical process but an emotional experience. And emotion can cloud our financial judgment and bring the best of us to ruin if we are not aware of what we are doing and the steps we need to take to control, or at least deal with, our financial foibles.

Human nature seems to have a genius for diverting us with emotional roadblocks when we should be driving straight ahead in accordance with our financial map for the future. For instance, many of us are actually afraid of having a lot of money because we're fearful of making an investment mistake and losing it all. Some of us use money as a weapon, and an unhappy spouse will overspend to get back at a partner. Still others of us keep all our savings in cash or in a bank account because we are worried we might not be able to get at funds when we need to. That accessibility, or liquidity, costs a lot and, in fact, can cause a shrinkage of capital as time goes by.

Quite often the more we earn the less we save because we think we must maintain a lifestyle commensurate with our job or career. Also our egos can get in the way and we won't admit that we don't know how to manage money. Other people automatically assume that we do know how since we have a nice home and a late-model car. (We assume the same of them.) But all of us are busy earning a living and busy trying to enjoy our spare time. Usually we're too busy to look after our own personal finances properly.

A budget won't necessarily protect you against your own emotional excesses. You might inadvertently exceed your expenses in a particular budget category. If you react to that emotionally rather than logically, you might decide that, since you've broken the contract with yourself, you might as well be in for a pound as a penny and go on a budget-breaking spending spree. If you are married or have a domestic partner, this could spark recrimination, anger and perhaps even revenge. A husband overspends on the weekend fishing trip so the wife decides to cut down on the family food budget. The husband is faced with TV dinners for a week until he's totally fed up and knuckles under or apologizes. As I have pointed out before, unless you control yourself, a budget can be like a diet — promising results for a while, then a surreptitious chocolate eclair, which in turn gives you an excuse to turf the whole project and go back to your normal, unreasonable but immediately satisfying eating habits.

Revenge (and Blackmail) in Personal Finances

Using money for revenge is a particularly common and corrosive way of dealing with money emotionally. If a family member perceives a personal slight he or she might feel fully entitled to go out and squander money on some long-savored but unnecessary item. Men sometimes use money to blackmail those they profess to love. If a woman is particularly pleasing to a man in some way, he might provide a financial reward — or withhold it, if she is not. Some parents use money to coerce and bribe their children. A mother might overspend at Christmas not because she is an especially giving person but to show what a good provider she is, and sometimes to buy the children's love. This may also happen at birthdays, graduations, christenings, first communions, bar mitzvahs and other special occasions.

None of these actions (and many others I haven't space to mention) is based on logic; all of them are emotional reactions. That's why money management is seldom the neat mathematical activity that every planner would like it to be — ask any couple.

What Is Your Money Personality?

Financial planning forces you to appraise yourself. To plan effectively, we must clearly define our motives and goals, put them down on paper and then build a plan based on them. But personal money management mirrors our very human and less-than-logical personalities. How we make or earn money, how we use it, how we save it and how we spend it very much reflects our emotional makeup. That is why sometimes insight from psychologists can be as important to us as we plan our financial future as the latest interest-rate forecast from a bank economist.

Psychologist Kathleen Gurney, Ph.D., tells us in her book *Your Money Personality* that "money is much more than an economic necessity. It is one of the most powerful motivators of human behavior."

"It taps into the deepest layers of our personalities and sets off powerful emotional charges," Dr. Gurney says. "Who you are and how you relate to money make the difference between working hard or working smart, struggling financially or living comfortably, making ends meet or feeling enriched, between poverty and wealth."

"Why does money seem to work so well in some people's lives yet act as a destructive force in others?" Dr. Gurney asks. "Do only the rich enjoy a sense of money satisfaction? Are the wealthy the only group that has learned to use money as a tool for happiness and contentment? Do you have to be a power seeker and a risk-taker in order to be financially successful? Why do some talented, creative, educated people end up on the bottom rung of the money ladder? How do men and women differ in their attitudes about money?"

These questions have never been fully addressed, she says, partly because the psychological and financial arenas seldom overlap. She adds that we know little about our "money selves" and the potent force that money has on all aspects of our lives. Dr. Gurney contends that "our confusing and paradoxical attitudes about money have set up a number of money traps from which we are unable to escape. At the same time we both condemn and worship money. These double messages are entrenched in every lifestyle, every profession, every personal relationship."

There is an "overabundance of books, seminars, and conferences on money strategies for getting rich, seeking money and power, climbing the corporate ladder," according to Dr. Gurney. "Yet none of the advice givers get to the root of the dilemma — making your emotional self work in harmony with your money self."

Dr. Gurney, who is president of Financial Psychology Corporation in Cincinnati, claims that to win at the money game you have to figure out how you fit into your country's financial picture. "Are you a money participant or a money spectator? Do your attitudes and feelings about money foster economic health or economic deprivation? Do you understand and implement the rules of the money game or are you playing by an old set of standards that sabotage financial liberation?"

To help clients make that assessment, Dr. Gurney developed a one-page questionnaire that determines a person's attitudes toward 13 financial traits that influence money behavior and investment decisions. She found after analyzing the responses to the questionnaire that most people use one of 9 distinct money styles: the Entrepreneurs, the Hunters, the High Rollers, the Safety Players, the Achievers, the Perfectionists, the Money Masters, the Producers and the Optimists.

Dr. Gurney reiterates, like so many others, that money cannot buy happiness. But it can be used constructively, she says, "as a tool to improve the quality of life, to increase the options in life, and to provide a sense of security and well-being. A true sense of mental wealth is attained when the following criteria are met:

1) You understand your money personality — how you relate to your money and how your attitudes affect your money behavior.
2) You neither exaggerate nor deny the importance of money.
3) Money is not viewed as an end in itself, but as a reward for achievement.
4) You control your money instead of letting it control you.
5) Money provides satisfaction and enjoyment as well as security."

She suggests that none of us can afford, financially or personally, "to take a passive approach to money. Like it or not, money can enhance happiness and posterity or it can destroy security and well-being. No one can drift to the pinnacle of success — you have to climb."

To be able to make that climb, you must discard a lot of emotional baggage along the way. Ultimately, she contends, money success comes from self-validation: as you think about your money self, so you become. Those who are willing to take an honest look at money truths, instead of camouflaging life with money myths and illusions, have a much better chance of achieving mental wealth.

The Best Defense Is to Know Yourself

I agree with Dr. Gurney's thesis — which I might sum up with the words "Know yourself." Managing your personal finances requires a lot of self-discipline, honesty and knowledge (both technical and psychological). Being emotional and impulsive can be an attractive personal trait sometimes — but not when it comes to money. If your basic approach to life is impulsive, you are not alone. Statistics indicate that most of us are impulsive, especially about money, and that we are therefore susceptible to current trends. We know that more than 90% of people are wrong when they follow trends, at least financial trends. They buy houses at the wrong time, when prices are high. They certainly buy stocks at the wrong time, also when prices are high. When prices fall a bit, the trend-followers panic and sell. This is completely irrational behavior and even if we know we are doing it, we keep repeating the same mistakes over and over.

Sometimes our impulsiveness can stem from the most positive roots. It's natural, for instance, to want to give our kids more in life materially than we ourselves had. Often we spare no expense to do that — financing their postgraduate studies or trips to Europe to gain experience. But we have to learn to temper such impulses with common sense. The good life, after all, does not consist of BMWs, winters in Gstaad, Gucci shoes, gold and silver place settings and crystal flutes filled with champagne — it boils down rather into the quality of our dealings with each other, the living and loving relationships we experience and must work to maintain.

Everyday Irrationality

An increasing number of articles and interviews appear in the media about the psychology of money, and with good reason. Money sometimes seems to bring out the emotional extremes in our personalities, even to lunatic limits. Financial advisors are increasingly asked to play psychologist with their clients while psychologists are logging a lot of hours, listening to their patients' financial woes. There probably is a touch of money madness in all of us, in varying degrees, and individual spending styles are rich in contradiction. One day you're cheerfully blowing $20 on a cab ride, the next you're switching off lights to save pennies on electricity. You carefully clip coupons to get a few cents off at the supermarket, then, while you're there, you'll walk over to the gourmet counter and pick out some caviar or Stilton cheese or smoked salmon as a treat.

Or you might think you're saving a little money by washing your own car. Then you jump in to it and charge off to the local auto store to buy some utterly useless gadget for it that represents far more than you saved washing it yourself all year.

The pages and reports in the media are regularly sprinkled with information about compulsive spenders: the average American consumer is spending at least 19% of his or her disposable income on debt. Or the staggering revelation that 30 million consumers are seriously overextended and using their credit to pay off credit, sucking themselves faster and deeper every month into a sweeping, downward spiral of debt. Many of these people, conclude a battery of "experts," suffer from chronic insecurity and shaky self-esteem. Perhaps that is why Americans spent something like $68 per month per capita on beauty products in 1988. In comparison, the amount spent on personal development and growth was less than 10 cents a month.

There is nothing wrong with spending money on yourself. You have to be good to yourself once in a while, perhaps more than once in a while. An article in the *Toronto Star* once cited a study that showed that high spending isn't necessarily a sign of high anxiety. In fact, apparently *controlled* extravagance can signal a personality that is healthier and happier than that of the relentless penny-pincher. That doesn't surprise me. I agree with the man who said that "the good life is expensive. There is another way to live that doesn't cost as much, but it isn't any good."

The Higher on the Ladder of Life, the Farther You Can Fall

Education and good jobs don't instinctively protect you from letting your emotions (mis)manage your financial life. It is common these days, for example, for large companies to make financial-planning advice available to senior executives. Corporations recognize the value of senior staff and know that, in many cases, these employees are overspending personally and need help. In fact, at all corporate levels a great deal of personnel-department consulting time is taken up with people whose money problems affect their job performances.

Many are continually hounded by creditors and in some cases wages are garnisheed. It would be interesting to see a study that measures the loss of employee effectiveness or time off the job that is directly attributable to poor personal money management. The corporate cost of assisting employees straighten out their financial problems is enormous.

Corporations are not alone in recognizing the problem of uncontrolled emotion affecting everyday judgment. Even religious counselors spend an inordinate amount of time counseling parishioners on financial matters. A few years ago the Canadian Council of Churches invested a substantial sum to develop a course to help the clergy counsel people on personal financial planning. The Council's surveys indicated that an increasing number of parishioners were turning to their priests or ministers in desperation, either for direct financial help from the coffers of the church, or for emotional release from frustrations caused by money problems.

Keeping Emotions and Finances Separate

How can you make sure your emotions don't control your financial life? First and foremost, of course, you should create a set of well-defined personal and financial goals. Around those goals you construct a personal financial plan. A plan in itself, of course, isn't enough. You also need to do a little soul-searching so that you can recognize the way you react to money emotionally. Then you have to fight your more destructive reactions. Sometimes a few special techniques can help.

If you are single, your work is cut out for you. If you are part of a couple, however, you must consider goals from another perspective as well. Here are some techniques that have helped me in this position:

Agree on Goals: One Way to Curb Emotional Money Management

A recurring problem peculiar to couples regarding their finances is the failure of the spouses to discuss at the most basic level what it is they are really trying to achieve with the money they save. One will automatically assume that the goals of the other are reasonable and in line with his or her own goals. After all, they love each other, don't they? But spouses' goals seldom match. It can come as quite a shock to learn just how far apart they can be. A husband is incensed that his wife doesn't understand that a new set of tires for the family car is absolutely vital and much more important than a new paint job for the kitchen. Sometimes disparate goals end up in compromise, which usually means that neither party gets what he or she wants. Compromise can often lead to resentment, and resentment is bound to surface eventually.

I'm told by one of the leading retirement counselors in Canada that the greatest problem he has to deal with among new clients approaching retirement age is getting them to agree on basic goals about handling their capital assets. A couple may have lived together most of their adult lives and they probably think they understand each other thoroughly. But the biggest problem they face when retirement looms is deciding how much of their capital is going to be converted into income. One spouse invariably feels that they should maximize income, even if that means that they might have to use up capital and thus reduce bequests to the children. The other spouse might feel they should cut back on their style of living and preserve their capital so all of it can be passed along to the offspring.

Develop Separate Wish Lists

That particular problem — income vs. asset protection — in some cases may have to end in compromise. But whenever possible, other differences of opinion about mutual goals should be resolved without resort to compromise. One way to do that is to make separate wish lists. Each spouse should draw up a list independent of the other. When you compare lists, conflicts should not be resolved by compromise. Rather, decide to achieve each spouse's top priority in parallel, at the same time. If that is impractical, then flip to see who goes first. Achieve that goal, uncompromised, then go after the other one. The second person might have to wait, but eventually both parties will get what they want and be happier for it. Most of us tend to be brought up in a family environment that teaches compromise. But compromise is not always the best approach; it often leads to nothing but disappointment for all concerned.

Don't Worry About the Neighbors

When I was young, my mother took in two university students as boarders. They were fine additions to the household and I thought they were there as company for me since my brothers were away. It was quite a while before I realized we had boarders out of economic necessity. If you start life without much money and you live in a less-affluent neighborhood than some of your friends, and everyone else around you is much the same, you have little reason to pretend your situation isn't other than what it is. You don't have to maintain a certain facade or keep up with the Joneses. But if you are accustomed to a certain standard of living most of your life and circumstances suddenly force you down a notch, you could find it difficult to face your friends and family. You might drop out of your health club because you feel you can't maintain a standard or hold your head high. Similarly, it's tough to move your kids from a private to a public school.

At times like this it is especially important to guard against emotions intruding on the management of your money. When you are down and depressed, you allow circumstances to worry you more than they should. For instance, when my father died, his life insurance helped pay off the fairly substantial mortgage on our home.

Even though it wasn't quite as necessary as before, my mother opened up the house to extra boarders. It made life a bit more comfortable for us. My mother found that easier to do than before because, as a widow, it was more socially acceptable for her to take in boarders. After all, that is what everybody expected a bereaved family to do in those days when its breadwinner died. A pretence of affluence was no longer needed.

I mention this because it is essential that all of us resist being stampeded by what others think, especially where money is concerned. There is no point trying to hold onto a position, a home or a car if you can't afford to, just because of pride. Accept economic reality. Then go to work to change it to what you want.

Women and Money

Attitudes are slowly changing, perhaps too slowly, regarding women and their independent need for money. Past generations did not teach women much about finances because good looks and manners were considered more important than education and financial prospects. A young woman was expected to make a good match. As Sophie Tucker said: "From birth to age eighteen, a girl needs good parents. From eighteen to thirty-five, she needs good looks. From thirty-five to fifty-five, she needs a good personality. From fifty-five on, she needs good cash."

Today it is absolutely essential that women receive every bit of education they can, if for no other reason than their chances of becoming single parents or family heads are much greater than they were a few short years ago. And if a woman has a happy and contented marriage, that union is likely to be even happier and more contented if she has her own source of income. And she should not be accountable to her husband or anybody else when she spends it.

The concept of couples doing everything together, having only joint bank accounts and discussing every savings and investment decision together needs critical examination. Despite conventional wisdom to the contrary, I think that these kinds of domestic arrangements can significantly contribute to marriage breakdown.

Everyone needs a certain degree of privacy, and that includes financial privacy. A married woman should have her own income. She should be accountable in the conventional sense for the way she spends joint household funds. But she should have some money that is entirely hers to do with entirely as she pleases, whether she works outside or inside the home. If the wife manages the home, she needs a budget for household operations, one that gives her leeway for some discretionary spending or saving. So, for that matter, should a husband if he is the homemaker. This is easier said than done sometimes, because usually in an emergency all family resources are thrown into the common pool. But the preservation of a happy partnership depends not just on openness between the parties but upon privacy between them as well.

To Each His (or Her) Own

This is easier said than done and it took me a long time to learn what I am now suggesting. In the early phases of my married life, money was so short that everything was pooled and joint major decisions had to be made almost every day as to how much we could spend on what. Eventually I realized this was grossly unfair to my wife. Yes, she did have the government family-allowance checks every month that she could spend as she saw fit. I paid the children's life insurance premiums to build up their future savings.

But she really needed more of her own money and she was not working outside the home. So, we decided that any checks coming into the house were hers to keep. These might be dividends or interest payments from investments that were not automatically reinvested, or family or anniversary gifts and so on. But it became apparent that we still hadn't gone far enough in providing her with her own income. About 10 years ago we decided that my wife's household allowance should cover food and minor clothing expenses, etc. Since I was the one working outside, I would look after all the capital expenditures, utilities, taxes, car payments and gasoline. Whatever she could save out of the household allowance was also to be hers to keep without having to account to anyone else.

This was the best move we ever made. The primary benefit was to involve my wife more in the family financial picture so she would less likely become a financial invalid. If one member of the family assumes the entire responsibility for finances and budgeting, the other member can soon develop what psychologists call "learned helplessness." Then, if a financial decision should go wrong, the uninvolved partner can shrug his or her shoulders and disclaim responsibility — perhaps not even feel inclined to participate in any solution. Many women today, especially older ones, become financially paralyzed when they are suddenly widowed, because they have never shared the responsibility for the family's money management. Many still have no idea of the extent of family assets, savings or even life insurance.

These women may not have been completely ignored during the family financial-planning process, but they had never had any ultimate responsibility or accountability. Fortunately this is gradually changing as younger women today are entering the workforce in greater numbers and assuming responsibility for their financial welfare.

My wife and I find the shared responsibility has brought us closer together. Sometimes we have fun with good-natured debates (at least *I* think they are) as to where expenses should fall: in my wife's budget or in mine.

At one time a few years ago I was advised by my wife that the purchase of my favorite bottle of Scotch was not to be considerd a household expenditure item, but rather a major capital expenditure to be paid for from my account. Sometimes we natter back and forth about whether an item is a minor household clothing expense (hers) or a major capital expense (mine). If we go on vacation for three weeks and I pick up the tab for all the expenses, I'm quick to point out to my wife that our household food budget has been mercifully spared that particular month, and that should warrant some reciprocal future budget consideration. It doesn't, and she refuses to discuss it.

Take Care of the Big Things: the Little Ones Follow

To sum up, the best protection against emotionally spawned financial excess is to recognize it can happen and to be constantly on guard. Develop and stick to a comprehensive financial plan that helps you take care of the essentials in life — the big-ticket items — by way of savings, or insurance, pensions, and so on. But build into your plan a little surplus so you have some latitude to indulge your emotions. After all, you are human. Nobody is perfect, and it takes a lot less effort to plan surplus into a budget than it does to try to control every emotion every day and perhaps change your entire basic behavior pattern.

So, go ahead and spend something on yourself. Make sure you build a little fun into your budget. Design it so that on your weekly sojourn to the supermarket for hot dogs for the barbecue you can *occasionally* stray into the deli area and toss a little smoked salmon or shrimp into the cart. Or so that you can try a six-pack of a new beer you've seen advertised. To assure yourself of a secure financial future you might have to cut down a bit on some of your wildest impulses. But you don't have to pinch pennies every minute, day and night.

6

Saving: The Foundation of Your Financial Plan

Obviously, an effective savings program is at the core of every successful financial plan. You build the rest of your plan on and around it. Without a savings program, there is no point in planning for financial independence.

Whether your personal goal is to retire early and travel the world, to take a full-time course in Chinese language and culture, to buy a bookstore, a house, a car or a gold watch, or simply to have more money than a dog has fleas, you have to be able to save consistently and effectively. But most of us can't. There is always something, some financial emergency, as we call it, that flashes forth unexpectedly to short-circuit our best savings resolutions. Haven't you, probably more than once, wistfully dreamed of an unanticipated inheritance from a distant and forgotten relative to help float you out of a financial backwater?

Perhaps you've dug your way inadvertently into a financial hole by buying too much on credit. You despair of ever being able to climb out of debt. So you throw up your hands at the futility of it all and spend even more money "to be good to yourself," and you hope for the best. Maybe you fantasize that you'll win the lottery. Well, consider the odds: 1 chance in 13,988,816 in 1988 for one popular lottery.

Even if you're in debt, that is no excuse not to save money. Every successful person as well as many unsuccessful ones owes money. Few of them pay off all their debts before they start to save. The intelligent planner, however, incurs debt by borrowing money to invest to make more money, not just to buy things. That's appropriate as long as you can service the debt properly and see growth in the investment. As a matter of fact, one of the few tax breaks the federal government has left us is the deductibility of interest on money borrowed for investment purposes.

And, of course, you borrow to buy a home through a mortgage. As you pay off the mortgage you are building equity in the house, a form of saving. The only caveat, again, is that the investment should appreciate more than the cost of servicing that debt.

It is sometimes wise to borrow money to make an RRSP contribution. We'll talk more about that in Chapter 9.

In a well-ordered world you'd pay off all your debts before starting to save. But we don't live in a well-ordered world. You almost always have outstanding credit-card debts in normal course of living. This should never prevent you from starting a regular savings program to provide for your future. The sooner you get started, the sooner the "miracle" of time and compound interest will start working to your advantage.

Everyone Can Do It

Forget the myth that you have to earn a lot of money to be able to save any. Don't believe for a minute that you have to take two years and many thousands of dollars out of your life to study for an MBA that will be your ticket to fortune. The way to accumulate any fortune, however modest, is to get your spending under control and to develop an effective and consistently applied savings program.

Everyone can do it. If the Waltons could, so can you. They were a couple who once attended our church when we lived in western Canada. I used to see them almost every Sunday and got to know them reasonably well. The husband was a caretaker of the local Legion Hall and he and his wife lived in a small apartment in the basement there. After service one Sunday I casually mentioned the concept of financial independence. They asked me to visit them so we could sit down and discuss some ideas about their financial futures.

Mr. Walton was not a prime prospect for life insurance, which I was selling at the time. His income was marginal and his wife did not have a paying job. They had no children whose education or future they had to worry about. However, Mr. Walton suffered from severe and prolonged epileptic seizures. For all practical purposes he was uninsurable. My company did offer some attractive savings programs designed to build financial independence for clients, but I had a lot of reservations as to whether the Waltons had enough discretionary income that they could put aside for the purpose.

When I arrived, the first thing that struck me was the apartment. It was small but beautifully kept, immaculately clean and highly organized. And my visit turned out to be a delightful, and surprising, one despite my original misgivings. Mrs. Walton made sandwiches and coffee and we sat around their tiny kitchen table. I outlined a savings plan that could work for them. They said they felt comfortable with what I was saying but I had to tell them that the plan was only a good one for them if they could make regular contributions to it for a fairly lengthy period of time. This was a long-term investment and the rates of return were attractive in those days when life was more orderly and the pace less rapid. I was apprehensive about their ability to handle continued contributions. I didn't want them to get hurt if they were forced to withdraw from the plan too early, before time and compound interest had a chance to work for them and build their savings to the amount they would eventually need.

No problem at all, they informed me, and explained why. Mr. Walton's job came with the apartment and a small monthly wage. That took care of their basic needs. And the Legion gave the Waltons the rights to all the empty pop bottles left in the hall every day and which Mr. Walton had to gather up when cleaning anyway. In those days each bottle carried a two-cent deposit, minimal as it was, but when they accumulated day after day it amounted to a reasonable sum every month. The Waltons intended to invest the bottle deposits in their future. He had no pension plan and they realized that his ability to work would not be guaranteed forever, so they wanted a plan that would take care of them when he could no longer work.

What made their story more remarkable was that Mrs. Walton was blind. Mr. Walton had a debilitating disease but he could hold down a job as a janitor. In those days she couldn't get a job but she maintained a beautiful apartment. I've never seen a happier and better attuned couple in all my life. I learned an important lesson from them: you don't have to earn a lot of money to save a lot, and there always seems to be a way if you look hard enough, even two cents per bottle. The Waltons' situation is similar to that of thousands of farm wives in those days who tucked the egg or milk money away in a teapot as their own independent source of income.

You could spend your entire life from age 20 dishing out hamburgers, fries and milkshakes at McDonald's, and still end up financially secure. You'd just have to put aside $20 a week in an RRSP (less than the cost of one night at the pub) and in 35 years you'd have saved $1,135,296, assuming your RRSP investment earned a return of 14.5% (a figure commonly used with mutual funds). If you decided to sling hamburgers for another five years to age 60, you'd retire with more than $2 million.

I know it's only too easy, especially if you are a low-wage earner, to fall into the rut of thinking you'll never be able to save enough money to become financially independent. But you can do it by changing the way you think about saving money if you want to badly enough. You prepare yourself properly by learning how to save — by reading books like this one, for example. The more you learn about saving, the more likely you are to realize that sometimes all you need is a slight change of focus in the way you look at things, a simple alteration of your fixed state of mind.

Consider, for example, what a slightly different perspective can do for you. Imagine you are offered a contract for a job of just 31 days. You can choose between two methods of payment: $1,000 a day for the 31 days, or start with one cent a day, which would double each of the remaining 30 days. Your first reaction probably would be to take the $31,000 and run directly to the bank. However, if you were to examine more closely the second payment option, you'd find that at the end of the month there would be $10,737,418.24 coming to you! It usually pays to look twice at the way you first react to apparent opportunities — a little shift of focus can often pay big dividends.

The Origins of the Money Jar

Let me tell you about an incident that first shifted my focus and led to a life of successful saving. In the summer of 1951 I was a young university student, approaching my last year. I was living in Winnipeg, 2,000 miles away from home, entirely on my own, and supporting myself with a construction job. I worked hard and played hard. The hard playing paid off when my partner and I won the city doubles tennis championships. The hard work paid off because I was putting aside enough money for my last year at college. The only flaw in my good life at that time was the fact that I never had been able to afford a wristwatch of my own.

I mentioned this to my landlady and her husband one evening, to excuse the fact that I had come in late for dinner. They said they might be able to help me. And they taught me two lessons I have never forgotten: one, that I could set an objective to achieve something I didn't think possible; second, that I could save money to buy a gold watch, or whatever else I might want.

The next day I came back to my room after work and found an empty quart sealer jar on my dresser, the old-fashioned glass jar our mothers and grandmothers used for canning vegetables and fruit. My part was simple. Every evening when I came home to get out of my work clothes, I was to empty my pockets of all my loose change and dump it into the jar. At first it didn't seem like I was getting very far. Some days there was only a dime or maybe a couple of nickels and a few pennies to drop into the jar. But other days would be better and a fair amount of change would clink into my preserve. Slowly, as the weeks went by, the level in the jar began to rise perceptibly. A few days before I was due to head back to school in Saskatchewan, my landlords and I sat around the kitchen table and I emptied the jar. After we had wrapped the coins for the bank I was amazed to learn that the total was $51 — a princely sum in those days.

Through my landlady's family, I was able to get a staff discount on a gold watch that was already on sale at Birks Ellis Ryrie. Because I could pay cash, I ended up with a $75 watch for $50. I have owned that watch proudly for more than 35 years and I never forgot that important financial lesson.

Since then I have learned that there are only two ways to acquire money: through people working and through money working. And there are only two kinds of people in the world: those who owe money and pay interest on it, and those who own money and earn interest on it. Ideally you will become one of those with money that works for you and earns interest, even when you are taking it easy.

Perhaps you've heard the old story about the bettor addicted to horse racing who headed out to the track with the comment, "I hope I break even today because I sure could use the money." Unfortunately, that punter reflects the saving habits of most Canadians today. Did you know that:

- 60% of all savings accounts that are opened in January are closed by the month of July.
- The average life of a savings account is 18 months and 5 days

from opening to closing.

- 85 out of 100 people alive at age 65 do not have as much as $250 in cash to spend as they wish.
- 90% of all deaths occurring after age 65 can be traced to financial worry.

I spend a great deal of time helping clients avoid becoming statistics like these. I help them develop balance sheets (net worth statements) and cash flow worksheets. I spend hours, even with computer assistance, working out elaborate personal financial plans for them that can fill as many as 20 to 45 pages of printouts. But no matter how detailed the plan, the question most often asked us is, "How do I get started? How can I save money consistently?"

The Three Basic Ways to Save Money

There are three ways to save money. The first way takes the form of the simple formula: subtract your expenses from your earnings or income, and save what is left.

Formula A:
In − Ex = S
INCOME − EXPENSES = SAVINGS (OR DEBT)

This is the approach (I deliberately don't call it a system) used by most people. Unfortunately it just doesn't work very well because, without a more sophisticated method to plot and control your spending, your expenses tend to run away with themselves and you have no way of knowing when to stop them short of your income. For too many people these days their expenses do exceed their income much of the time. When that happens, they often start borrowing both long and short term just to keep up with their spending, just "to bridge the gap." I wish I had a dollar for every time a client of friend ruefully tells me that, "It's not that my income is too small; it's just that the month is too long."

And this way of trying to save doesn't take into consideration unexpected expenses. Like a sudden, silent avalanche, the unforeseen outlay is what buries us financially. It may take the form of replacing the worn broadloom in your home, a new set of tires for the car or an urgent summons to attend a seriously sick parent in the Outer

Hebrides. Whatever it is, you can't anticipate it and there is no contingency in the income-minus-expenses formula to cover it. As Charles Dickens' Mr. Micawber once graphically put it: "Annual income twenty pounds, annual expense nineteen nineteen six, result happiness. Annual income twenty pounds, annual expenditure twenty pounds ought and six, result misery."

Another way to save is to pay yourself first and then live on what is left.

Formula B:
In − S = Ex
INCOME − SAVINGS = EXPENSES

This is not a bad formula and it can work for many people. At the very least it points you in the right direction, though it doesn't result in a savings program fine-tuned for your particular needs. Nor does it prepare you for some of the financial vicissitudes in your future. But you *can* use this formula, and you can do so without seriously restricting your lifestyle. You soon learn to adjust what is left after you first deduct your savings.

One of the problems with Formula B and Formula A is a hidden virus they contain that can knock your savings plan off its feet month after month. It uses a false name, appearing on your monthly list of expenditures as "miscellaneous." It's not unusual to fritter away $300, $400 or even $500 every month on items you just cannot account for. Because there is no other category in your expense budget, you enter the cash you dribble away during the month (if you are keeping track) under "miscellaneous." Check it out. For a full week, keep track of every penny you spend. You'll find the "miscellaneous" column mounts up only too quickly. You have a beer or two after work, a midweek night out on the town, a pair of shoes that takes your fancy and you buy a couple of extra lottery tickets. It adds up faster than you think and usually you just can't remember where it went. When you are able to rein in your runaway miscellaneous expenses, you are halfway to winning the savings race.

Another major drawback to the save-first-and-live-on-the-rest formula is that you never know exactly how much you should be saving first. If you take too big a savings bite from your income every two weeks you could end up with financial indigestion that could upset your lifestyle too much. The old adage "All work and no play" should not be taken lightly. The result at best can be dullness, all right, but budget burnout is just as likely.

On the other hand if you save too small a bite, a year from now, 5 years or 20 years hence, you could face financial starvation. Balance is what you seek. One of my colleagues has coined a phrase about the balance we seek: "Plan for tomorrow. But live for today."

So, if you seek financial security, you must move beyond Formula B. You must come up with the answer to the question of how much you really need to save. How much should you take off the top of each paycheck and salt away before you spend a cent? It's not an easy job to find out, but you have to. In fact, what you have to do is *develop a comprehensive personal financial plan.* Your plan will document what you want to accomplish in life and the goals you have set. These might include the amount of income you would like to have at retirement, and how much income you think your family will need if you should die prematurely or suddenly become disabled. Through your plan you will anticipate how much you'll need to cover further education for yourself at some point or your children's education or for a downpayment on a house. It will record how often you are likely to buy a new car and how much you will spend on vacations. Unless you look to the future and make a stab at putting a price or cost on what sometimes seems an unlimited number of possible expenses, you'll never actually know how much you have to save today. Preparing a personal financial plan is the only way to answer the question, "How much is enough?"

Formula C:
G + B = FF
GOALS + BUDGET = FINANCIAL FREEDOM

That brings us to the third formula: you establish a set of personal financial goals. You develop a budget to help you reach those goals. You follow the formula faithfully, and eventually you find financial freedom.

I can hear you now, moaning, "Goals! How can I set goals? I've never been goal-oriented."

But goal-setting is essential if financial freedom is your ultimate objective. As writer and editor Gloria Steinem said, in an interview in *Cosmopolitan* magazine, about her goal-less life before she matured: "I didn't think about goals . . . . The degree to which you can control your future makes you more aware of how much power you have. Rich people plan for three generations; poor people plan for Saturday night."

Well, setting financial goals is not really that difficult, especially if you have a checklist or guidelines to help you. And a budget can make your goals attainable.

That Terrible Word

Budgeting! The word has nasty connotations. Nobody likes to budget. Budgeting smacks of self-denial, austerity, drabness and routine. It conjures up images of bare subsistence and "doing without." And it requires a substantial allotment of that quality so much in demand by most of us but so little in evidence: self-discipline. There must be another way.

There isn't. Successful budgeting takes a lot of work, a lot of self-discipline and a lot of practice. Trying to build a solid successful financial plan unless you have constructed a sound budget to base it on first is as useless as laying out a building lot on quicksand — whatever you build will slowly and surely sink away. But you'd be surprised what capabilities are hidden deep within yourself once you decide that financial freedom is what you really want. And it's a lot easier to budget when you know there is plenty of help available and you don't have to handle the whole job yourself.

A sensible budget for someone who wants financial autonomy is as necessary as a sensible diet for the 300-pounder who wants freedom from physical ailments later in life, or simply next week. Saving money is often compared to dieting or quitting smoking. But the comparison is not really valid. If you start a diet and then fall off the food wagon before you reach your weight-loss goal, you can always start over again. I know because I've done it. I've lost hundreds of pounds in my life. And I've also put every one of them back on.

It's the same with trying to break the cigarette habit: if you quit smoking but two weeks later you're back puffing your way through two packs a day because it's the only way to banish the screaming meemies, you still can take another run at putting the nicotine habit behind you anytime you summon up enough discipline to start again. It's true that your health probably has suffered during those intermittent smoke-filled periods of shattered resolve, but even that can be improved.

Unlike dieting and kicking the smoking habit, however, once you stop following your budget you can never make up for the spending binge you go on. You can never replace the money you didn't save when you were off-budget. You earn only a certain amount of money in your lifetime. When you squander some of it, it's like oil from Alberta. Once you spend some of that nonrenewable resource, it's gone for good and you can't get it back.

I often tell clients that "a fortune will flow through your hands during your working life. What you will have to show for it will depend on your ability to manage and control your money."

That's easier said than done. A study of 600 Metropolitan Toronto area people, conducted for the *Toronto Star* newspaper by Goldfarb Consultants in 1987, underlines that fact. The study revealed that the single greatest frustration during the previous 5 years for these people aged 25 to 40 was their personal finances. By 2 to 1 their concern about money matters outstripped worries about their two next most vexing frustrations: work- and children-related problems. I've found the same concern in my own business. During the day many of our clients worry about money sitting up; at night they fret lying down. They fear an avalanche of unpaid bills triggered by their helter-skelter recordkeeping. And they stew about their nonexistent savings and a budget that simply does not recognize reality.

Often our fears of a lucre-less future arise not from fact but from misunderstanding facts or not knowing how to deal with the facts. We have a limitless number of excuses for not managing our money: "It's too complicated," or "too time-consuming," or "too technical." What we really are saying is "I'm scared stiff," or "I really don't know how to do it."

It's not so difficult to overcome your fear and misunderstanding of saving and managing money and to get your financial act together — when you know where to get help. The Money Jar approach is to help you generate confidence in your ability to manage your financial affairs by starting slowly, taking one step at a time. Learn and master the initial, relatively simple concepts before moving on to more sophisticated levels of money management. Why not begin right now?

Step Number One

Start your budgeting with a single, simple activity that works, one that will prove to you that you can do it without suffering any financial hardship. Remember the Money Jar that started me on the way to a life of saving? You follow the same path. Take all the loose change from your purse or pocket every night and put it into your Money Jar on the dresser. Use a coffee tin, or whatever, if you haven't got a jar. You'll soon find that saving your change doesn't curtail your lifestyle noticeably. You probably won't miss it at all. After 30 or 60 days you will be amazed at how much you have accumulated. This relatively effortless act of saving loose change is a simplified version of Formula B, paying yourself (or saving) first and spending what is left. Psychologists tell us that it takes only 27 days of repetitive activity to form a habit. If you resolutely drop your change into the jar for at least 27 days running, then you have started the saving habit. Once you have developed the habit, then, the odds are that you'll likely continue it.

When you've proven the value of the Money Jar to yourself you can slowly beef up your daily deposits by moving to an alternating pattern of loose change one day and a dollar bill or loonie the next. Once you think you can handle that, take the next small step and increase the denomination of the banknote you tuck away. You'll be delighted at how quickly the total accumulates. When I was a child there used to be an old saying, "Tuck away a buck a day." A buck a day doesn't seem like much but $365 dollars a year earning interest at a modest 10% per year grows steadily into $66,044 in 30 years. At 12% it would blossom forth at $98,655. Not bad for just a buck a day, with no decline in your style of living.

Should You Do as the Babylonians Did?

If you decide not to bother with planning your financial future any further, you can take the next (and last) Formula B step: adopt an old theory that goes back to ancient Babylon (and forget about reading the rest of this book). The theory has it that each payday if you pay yourself first, before any of your creditors, the amount of 10% of what you earn, you eventually will become financially independent. So the first 10% of every paycheck you bring home is yours to keep (in this case, save); the rest you are free to spend. It's a simple formula and it can work. If you invest that 10% wisely and don't touch it over a long period of time you will undoubtedly become financially independent some day. But what day?

As far as I am concerned, you need more than a simple 10% formula to cope effectively today because life is a little more complicated now than it was in ancient Babylon. As I mentioned before, you have no way of knowing whether saving 10% is too much or too little. That depends on many things, including your age and your personal goals. If you stop at Formula B you might find that someday you have saved enough. Or you might not. You certainly won't have developed an integrated financial plan, and you won't necessarily have protected your savings against unanticipated disasters. The only way to weave an assured financial security blanket is to move to Formula C.

Budgeting — the Easy Way

A proper financial plan, of course, forces you to think about and establish goals and to develop plans to achieve them. A financial plan helps you protect what you do accumulate in your savings program. And if a savings program is at the core of every successful financial plan, then a budget is at the center of every successful savings program. From students whose money often runs out before the end of the month to executives with 6-figure incomes, everyone needs a budget. It's almost axiomatic that the more money you earn, the less you are able to account for how you spend it. And if you can't do that, one day you'll look up and find you've spent more than you've earned.

A budget is a simple process to help you keep your expenses in line with your income. But always remember that the most sophisticated budget is not a financial plan — it is only one of the tools to help you carry out your financial plan. Nor will setting up a budget mean you automatically will save a vast fortune. You are the one who has to save. You are the one who must make the decisions. A budget helps you organize your decision-making; a budget won't make bank deposits. Some eager savers start off by setting up an extensive, sophisticated budget and are determined to live and die according to that budget. They try to account for every penny they spend during the month. They expect to dot every *i* and cross every *t*. But that is a strenuous exercise and in most cases it is futile and unnecessary.

If you have a partner and possibly a family and try to adhere rigidly to an intricate and sophisticated budgeting system, this will usually cause strife among the other people affected by it. In a family, such a budget usually originates with one peson and others are forced to agree with it. This kind of unilateral budget is a win/lose proposition, and when a win/lose situation exists within a family or couple, invariably everybody loses.

If you want to improve your physical condition, you don't start with the exercises on the last page of the program. You start slowly, with a simpler, less-demandng workout until you are ready to move on to the next step. It's the same with budgeting. Start slowly, stay within your level of ability to understand the process, and the time you have available. A few hours each month over, say 3 months, devoted to considering your income and your expenses gives you enough time to gradually reduce overspending, free up money for savings and investments and build a cash reserve for emergencies and opportunities.

Building a Budget — Month One

For the first month keep track of how much money comes in and, more importantly, how much goes out. Jot your figures down on two separate pieces of paper; call them your daily ledger. You don't need to be precise to the last penny when you note expenses, just round the figures out. And don't try to keep track of every last package of chips or chocolate bar as you tote up your weekly food bill. The idea is to determine approximately how much you spend for food. Is it $200 a month or $500?

That's all you do in Month One. If you find it is not a very typical month, so far as expenses go, you could continue the process for another month, although that's probably not necessary because you'll find there is no such thing as a typical month.

Building a Budget — Month Two

This month you prepare your actual budget (or cash flow) worksheet. The first step is to develop a format sheet with the appropriate income and expense headings. If you like, you can use the form given here. (*See Figure 3.*) Whatever format you use, make at least 12 copies. You will want to fill one in each month to keep track of your income and expenses.

CASH FLOW STATEMENT

INCOME FROM EMPLOYMENT	Client	Spouse	A/M*
**Net Salary	______	______	____
—Commissions	______	______	____
—Self Employment	______	______	____
—Other	______	______	____
INVESTMENT INCOME			
—Interest	______	______	____
—Dividends	______	______	____
—Rent (net of cash expenses)	______	______	____
—Annuities & Pension Income	______	______	____
—Government Benefits	______	______	____
—Spousal & Child Support	______	______	____
—Other	______	______	____

BASIC EXPENDITURES			
—Housing	—Mortgage or Rent	________	____
	—Property Taxes	________	____
	—Property Insurance	________	____
	—Heat, Hydro & Water	________	____
	—Property Maintenance	________	____
	—Other Housing Costs	________	____
—Food		________	____
—Clothing		________	____
—Transportation	—Loan Payment/Rent	________	____
	—Insurance	________	____
	—Fuel	________	____
	—Maintenance	________	____
	—Other Transportation	________	____
—Telephone		________	____
—Household Expenses	—Improvement/Purchases	________	____
	—Cleaning/Help	________	____
—Education		________	____
—Recreation & Club Membership		________	____
—Personal Care & Improvements		________	____
—Health Care & Insurance	—Medicare	________	____
	—Health Ins.	________	____
	—Life Ins.	________	____
	—Disability Ins.	________	____
	—Other Ins.	________	____
—Loan Repayments	—Investment Assets	________	____
	—Personal Assets	________	____
	—Credit/Charge Cards	________	____
	—Other Debts	________	____

—Charitable Donations		________	____
—Discretionary Expenditures	—Entertainment	________	____
	—Vacations	________	____
	—Gifts	________	____
	—Support	________	____
	—Retirement	________	____
	—Investments	________	____
	—Savings	________	____
	—Personal Allowance	________	____
	—Other	________	____

* A = Annual *M = Monthly
**Net of UIC/CPP and income tax deducted at source.

Figure 3: Cash-flow statement. You can use this one or tailor it to suit your particular circumstances.

The next step is to add up all your expenses for a year, category by category, so you can fill them in on the cash flow worksheet. To do this you will use some of the figures you jotted down during Month One. Also, you must gather together all your records from the past year. These include items such as paycheck stubs, canceled checks, credit-card statements, bills, sales receipts, tax returns and bank books.

Try to keep all these records in one place. An easy way to do this is to buy a small cardboard or metal file drawer, perhaps an accordion file, at your local stationer or office-supply store. Also get a few manila file folders into which you can slip your receipts and paid invoices. Label the folders with the same headings you use on your budget worksheet so that at the end of the month, or year, it will be easier to put your hands on each category of expense or income and add it up.

Category by category, add up all your expenses to find out how much you spent during the last year. Divide each category's total by 12 to get an average monthly expense, and enter those figures on the budget worksheet. You are preparing a monthly average budget here. Your actual expenses will almost always be above or below the averages shown on your budget worksheet for any given month, but by year-end, if you have stuck to your budget, the final totals should match those on the worksheet. For instance, if you took a summer vacation last year and it cost $1,000 in total, then it should go in your cash flow worksheet as $1,000 divided by 12, or about $85 per month. Do the same with Christmas expenses, or car-insurance payments or whatever lump-sum payments and expenses occur throughout the year.

Preparing a budget like this is the way you anticipate those unexpected expenses that come up from time to time. Usually it's not the day-to-day costs that strain a budget, but the bills you forgot were coming. You have to include them in your budget so you can plan for them.

Now you have your budget worksheet filled in. What you are looking at should represent your financial reality. The next step is to assess whether you have to adjust that reality so you can save something each month.

By the way, one of the biggest problems you'll face in developing a budget worksheet like this is missing records. You must keep all receipts and records relating to income and expenditures, even notes authorizing prepayments or automatic deductions from your bank account or paycheck. I have found that the biggest gap in my clients' records comes from the way they handle cash. If you receive cash income from a source, make sure you don't use it as your personal allowance for the month — deposit all the cash you receive in the bank, and write a check to yourself for that allowance. That way you will have all your expenses (and income) recorded in your checkbook, and that checkbook will be the single most important source of recorded expenses and income. The same goes for your paycheck — deposit it in the bank, then write yourself a check for personal expenses. If you don't do this, too much unrecorded cash can slip through your fingers and will never be incorporated into your budget. And your budget will never balance.

Building a Budget — Month Three

In the third month carefully evaluate your budget worksheet to make sure you can live with the expense and income levels on it. If you have underestimated your expenses or neglected to add a cost category, correct it now. You can personalize the worksheet format if you want, to include other expense or income categories that reflect your personal circumstances. But now is the time to adjust your budget if it does not balance.

You will want to see a reasonable amount in the savings category. Shoot for 10% of your net income if you can, until you have more time and more knowledge to assess how much you really need to save. If your budget shows you don't have enough left over to save after expenses, you'll have to revise your spending patterns. With all your income and expenses on paper in front of you, it is relatively easy to determine where you are overspending and where you should make adjustments.

The expense category that can throw your budget out of whack, of course, is the never-never land known as "miscellaneous." On the cash flow worksheet "Miscellaneous" is really the two subcategories labeled "Other" and "Personal Allowance" under the general heading of "Discretionary Expenditures." If they are, you must get a better handle on your monthly expenses by jotting down every penny you spend for a month or two, as you spend it, in a daily journal. Sometimes that "spending journal" is needed the first few months you get serious about budgeting. This will help you plug the leaks that otherwise can drown you financially.

Spend an hour or two each week during that third month studying your expense categories and trying to trim any excess you find. That way you can build up your savings and investment categories. For instance you might find that you are spending $150 a week going out for dinner. That amounts to about $7,500 a year. If, instead, you were to contribute that $7,500 each year to your RRSP and get a modest yield of 10%, you'd be a millionaire twice over in 30 years. The enjoyment you'd miss by not dining out would be more than offset by the satisfaction of knowing that one day you'll have a fund of more than $2,200,000 tucked away. With that behind you, you could spend the rest of your life dining out in the best restaurants around the world.

But I'm not suggesting that you stop eating out. You could, however, try a less expensive restaurant every second week and cut your costs by $50 or so every month. Even a contribution of $600 a year to an RRSP at 10% would grow to $108,566 in 30 years.

Spending Guidelines

Here are some guidelines you can use to assess your budget. Compare what you spend with what the experts say you should.

- Allocate 65% of your take-home pay for fixed expenses including rent or mortgage payments, utilities and food.

- Spend no more than about 30% on mortgage payments or rent. Two-income families with higher earning power perhaps might lay out up to 33 ⅓ %. This is certainly true in overheated real-estate markets such as those in Toronto and Vancouver.
- Allow 20% for variable outlays such as household repairs, recreation and clothing.
- Put aside 10% for insurance premiums and property taxes.
- Save that remaining 5% (at least). If you are a two-income family, each of you should save at least 5% of each paycheck. If your take-home pay exceeds $1,200 a month each, your fixed expenses will probably be less than 65% of the total and each of you should be able to save up to 10% of your income.
- If you use 10% or less of your after-tax income to pay off credit cards and other charge-account bills, you are not in bad shape. If that figure creeps to, or beyond, 15%, you are starting to lose the battle of the budget. At 20% you'd better leave those cards at home, regardless of what the advertisements say.

Have Trouble Sticking to Your Budget? Here Are Some Ideas That Might Help

Don't be too hard on yourself. Like so many other things in life, successful budgeting depends on balance and reason, on being neither too rigid nor too lax. If you like to do certain things, by all means do them. But make adjustments in other areas of your budget so you can still save. It's only too easy to undo all your best intentions by becoming too picky with yourself and with your spouse or partner if you have one. A good budget should be a positive element in your life, not a negative one. It is just a tool to help you shape a good life for yourself and your family; it shouldn't hang over your head like the sword of Damocles. It must serve you; you must not become a slave to it. Remember the primary purpose of a budget is to generate extra cash at the end of each month for you to save and invest. Your goal of financial independence is relatively long term. "What's the good of money if you can't have a little fun with it?" writer/reformer Nellie McClung once said. She had the right idea.

Use frequent and continuous positive reinforcement. One way to do that is to keep very close track of your progress. When you make a monthly deposit to one of your savings accounts at the bank, take the time to line up and do it personally. Avoid electronic transfers or overnight deposit slots. When you make the deposit, have your passbook brought up to date while you wait. You'll have more incentive to keep saving when you see the total growing each month from your deposits and the interest they earn. You don't get nearly as much positive reinforcement if you bring your bank book up to date only a couple of times a year.

There is no reason you can't be a bit corny about positively reinforcing your savings achievements. For instance when my son received his first paycheck from his first job, we took a couple of pictures of him proudly brandishing that check. When he opened his bank account, I took a photo of the bankbook showing 10% of his earnings as the first deposit. It all helps. You might even want to frame those photos and hang them on your wall.

Schedule quarterly reviews. At least every three months sit down and review the growth in all parts of your savings program. I keep a folder in my desk that contains an analysis of nearly all my holdings. Use an informal ledger format on a piece of foolscap — the various bank accounts, mutual funds, Canada Savings Bonds and other savings vehicles across the top of the page, and the four review dates down the side. Fill in the line across. If you have Canada Savings Bonds, do a rough calculation of how much interest income has been added during the quarter. Add your various current bank balances plus interest. Note the value of your mutual funds, or stocks, from the business pages of the newspaper, and add those. If you have life-insurance policies with a savings component, add those too. Then add up the entries across the page to get a grand total of your current savings position. You will be tremendously encouraged when you find that your savings have increased perhaps $500 or $1,000 in the past three months.

The file is useful for another reason. If I'm ever tempted to stop or cut down contributions or to spend some of these savings, I pull it out and look at the growth. It always cools my spending ardor.

Prepare a personal net worth statement (balance sheet) at the end of the year. This is a more comprehensive survey than you did each quarter and it provides you with a snapshot of your current total financial worth on the date you prepare it. You can use the balance sheet in *Figure 4* if you like. You include all the categories you used in your quarterly savings review and add others. The equity in your house if you own one, and how much it has increased during the year, would be one to add. It's not difficult to estimate the current value of the house by finding out, perhaps through a friendly real-estate agent, what comparable house prices are in your neighborhood. A house is probably your most valuable asset and you don't want to leave it out of your calculations. Add to your equity the amount you have paid down (principal) on your mortgage during the year.

NET WORTH STATEMENT (BALANCE SHEET)

LIQUID ASSETS	**Client**	**Spouse**
—Cash	__________	__________
—Short Term Deposits	__________	__________
—Cash Sur. Value Life Ins.	__________	__________
—Other	__________	__________
INVESTMENT ASSETS		
—Term Deposits	__________	__________
—Mutual Funds	__________	__________
—Stocks	__________	__________
—Bonds	__________	__________
—Tax-Inc. Investments	__________	__________
—Real Estate Investments	__________	__________
—Business Interest	__________	__________
—Other	__________	__________
—RRSP	__________	__________
—Emp. Pension Plan	__________	__________
—DPSP	__________	__________
PERSONAL ASSETS		
—Residence	__________	__________
—Vacation Property	__________	__________
—Household Furnishings	__________	__________
—Art, Antiques & Collectibles	__________	__________
—Clothing, Furs & Jewelry	__________	__________
—Automobiles	__________	__________
—Other	__________	__________

SHORT TERM OBLIGATIONS (LIABILITIES)		
—Charge Account/Credit Cards	____________	____________
—Personal Loans	____________	____________
—Accrued Taxes (Personal & Property)	____________	____________
—Other	____________	____________
LONG TERM OBLIGATIONS		
—Mortgage (residence)	____________	____________
—Loans on Investment Assets	____________	____________
—Loans on Personal Assets	____________	____________
—Other	____________	____________

Figure 4: Balance sheet, or net worth statement. Fill it out. Then subtract your total obligations from your total assets. You might be pleasantly surprised.

Don't forget to add the current value of your pension fund or your RRSP by including your contributions for the year.

The total of all your assets including your savings should balance the total of all your short- and long-term liabilities. If you compare it with the previous year's balance you will be able to see the progress you have made during the year. There is no greater encouragement to persist with your savings game plan, or even intensify them, than an obvious growth in your balance sheet values.

By the way, it's a good idea to start thinking about the money your savings program generates as "capital" and forget the "pool" designation. Capital is an asset, and you tend to protect an asset against shrinkage and usually expect it to grow over time. And grow it will, because, if properly managed, an asset works for you, earns interest and grows, even when you sleep. "Them that has, gets," the old adage goes, and it's true. If you nurture an asset, it will flourish.

On the other hand, when you think of your savings as one big pool, you tend to treat it as a discretionary accumulation of money you can dip into whenever you like. When you use the mental label "savings pool," two things usually happen. First, when you run into an emergency, or temptation overwhelms you and you can't resist buying that new compact-disk player or a sure-fire penny stock touted by a friend who "knows" it's going to quadruple in four weeks, your accumulated pool starts to drain away — you dissipate what you don't recognize as an asset and the prospects of eventual financial freedom become arid indeed. Second, because you have not identified specifically what you are saving for, you tend to keep your money liquid. That means it sits in a savings account at the bank and earns a relatively low rate of interest because you think you might want to get at it quickly in the event of emergency (or unbearable temptation). A savings pool seldom rises much above its original level. In fact, chances are that when taxes and inflation start to work on it, your "pool" begins to dry up and the level of your savings pool's actual buying power actually drops. So, your budget is intended to build up your capital and your assets.

A Family Affair

If you are part of a family unit, make sure that budgeting is a family affair, with all members involved in the planning process. Husbands and wives should both be involved in the recordkeeping as well as the preparation of a budget, regardless of who is paying the bills. Finances should always be discussed jointly. After all, one of the spouses might not always be around, and the other must be in a position to carry on the process. Even your children should be aware that you are operating within a budget. That can keep them from pestering you about some items they would like to have, whether a new bicycle or a new dress or whatever.

Finally, there is a sensible rule to follow for budgeting in general: if balancing your income and outflow is to become a habit, you need to make sure you design a program that is easy to live with.

Here Are a Few Tips to Help You Persist With Your Budget

Many people lose the battle of the budget when they take on too much, too suddenly. They become discouraged and quit. For instance, it usually is not reasonable to expect that you'll save 10% of your earnings and at the same time manage to reduce your instalment debts from 25% to 15% of your takehome pay. But, when you finally create a realistic, livable budget, you know that you will reach your financial goals in due course, and your sense of satisfaction and self-esteem will soar.

- If you find that your budgeting resolve is starting to weaken and your expenses are getting a little out of hand, don't be too hard on yourself. Recognize that a budget is mainly a direction, designed to start you down the road you want to follow. You don't always walk or run at the same speed. So you shouldn't expect always to save at exactly the same rate. The main thing is to try and stick with it, even if you stray off the beaten path from time to time. Jumping off the cliff is not the alternative to straying off your budget's track.
- If you tend to be an impulse buyer, be sure to keep the cash you carry with you to a minimum. It might be inconvenient at times, but it sure helps prevent you from overspending. If you don't carry much cash, it can't burn a hole in your purse or pocket.
- Don't apply for a number that permits you to use your bank's automatic-teller machines. That makes it too easy to abuse your bank account. If you have to spend time and line up at the bank to get cash from a human teller, you won't bother as often and you'll make do with less cash on hand. Automatic-teller machines can be savings slayers, especially on Sundays.
- This is not an original thought, but it bears repeating: one of the best ways to save money on the food budget is to shop only after eating, when you are not hungry. Otherwise all sorts of unneeded nachos and snacks seem to find their own way into the shopping cart. If you are male and have to do your own shopping, make a list only of what you need. And buy a set of blinkers to use in the store. Men seldom make out a shopping list in advance and stick to it as women are apt to do. If you are like me in the supermarket, you can resist anything but temptation. If you can afford it, fine yourself if you stray from your list.
- One of the rules we follow in our house is that all checks that arrive in the mail, regardless of whether they are interest payments, dividends, birthday gifts, refunds or whatever, go into a savings account at the bank or trust company. Try not to spend check money. That also goes for family allowance (baby bonus) checks — but we will deal with those in another chapter. Putting all checks in the bank makes recordkeeping easier, too.

- Consistency is a secret to successful saving. It is easier to save if you divert predetermined sums to various savings accounts with the same regularity and fidelity that you pay the rent or mortgage. A variation on this theme if you are employed is to have money taken out of your paycheck before you ever see it and automatically transferred to a savings account through payroll deduction.
- If you get a salary increase at work, save it all if you can, instead of raising your expense or spending level.
- When you pay your expenses at the end of the month, try this: round out the entries you make in your check register. For instance, if you write a check for $76.25, enter it in the check register as $80. When you write your monthly mortgage or rent check (or even if you have authorized automatic deductions from your bank account) of say $722.49, deduct $730 or even $750 from the running total in your register. In other words always put down more than what the check actually is. It's a bit more difficult to balance your account when your statement comes, but you can get the hang of it fairly quickly. If you do this with all or most of your checks you will find that at month-end you've got a lot more money in your account than what shows in the register. Then you transfer that extra amount into a savings account.

Strive for balance — balance in saving and balance in spending. If you are a spendthrift, you become a victim of money. If you are too frugal, you are also a victim. Use money wisely. Spend it to comfort yourself and others, and don't comfort yourself with the process of accumulating it. The love of money is not necessarily the root of all evil. It depends whether you use it solely for selfish purposes, or sometimes for the benefit of others.

Above all, don't look upon saving money as an end in itself. Do you remember the adage about money not bringing happiness? That old saw perpetuates another myth about money that is patently silly. It makes about as much sense as saying that a home freezer is not a good form of transportation. Money was never intended to buy or bring happiness. It is intended to bring comfort, and if you are miserable, at least you can be miserable in comfort.

In many respects I think life is like a big Monopoly game: when the time comes to depart this life we merely pass on the properties and the cash and somebody else will use them to play the game after we've gone. Money is just here for us to use, like many of the other material things in life. After all, you can't take what you accumulate with you.

7

Spending: The Ultimate Seduction

Little wonder many of us fail to achieve our financial goals — we are surrounded by armies of skilled marketing professionals whose sole purpose is to entice us, persuade us and encourage us to spend our money. They play on our hopes, fears, and greed, but mostly on our egos.

Marketers have convinced us that the human body was never more in need of preventatives, preparations and cosmetics to make sure we don't become social outcasts. Banks, trust companies and other financial institutions have made it so easy to borrow or use credit cards with little regard to repayment or costs that self-help groups modeled on Alcoholics Anonymous have been springing up around the country as havens for those who feel their lives are being ruined by debt. It's not difficult to believe a top executive from a U.S. non-profit credit-counseling foundation when he claims that 30 million Americans were having financial difficulty in 1989.

Since most of us are unschooled in money management and unprepared to withstand the endless enticement of the marketing message, we often succumb: we spend instead of save. Against this formidable marketing foe we all need a little help so that our hopes for a comfortable retirement don't slowly swirl away in a sinkhole of superfluous spending.

But it isn't easy. That rather daunting throng of trained marketing professionals — in advertising, public relations, market research and ancillary fields — spend their days and sometimes nights plotting to weaken our will to save. They use every conceivable research and planning technique to devise subtle strategies to get us to spend. Ours is a materialistic society and the marketing professional has had a powerful hand in shaping consumers' attitudes. Marketing is highly developed, almost a science in the way it can predict cause and effect, and a lot of intelligent people fill its ranks. They are not in any way malevolent and both they and we participate wholeheartedly in the legitimate enterprise of selling and buying. So, it is up to each one of us to be aware of the constant marketing pressures exerted on us and to resist those pressures when we have to. And we do have to more often than not.

Scene 1: Behind the Scenes at Amalgamated Foods Limited

We are silent observers of a hastily called marketing meeting at this fictitious giant supermarket chain.

> V-P MARKETING: All right, people. We have a serious situation here and that's why I've called you together. This marketing team has got to come up with some answers and come up with them fast. The executive vice-president called me on the carpet this morning after he looked over our monthly competitive analysis. It seems that Amalgamated has lost 1½ points market share of popcorn store sales. Popcorn is one of our big profit items, as you know, and we can't afford to lose market share, particularly to those guys across the street at Premium Foods. So, let's knuckle down and put our thinking caps on together to see how we can get those points back.
>
> MARKET RESEARCHER: I've got an idea, boss. Why don't we survey our customers coming out of, say, a half a dozen stores? That should help us find out why they aren't buying popcorn the way they did before. I can do another survey in front of Premium's stores to find out why their popcorn sales are up. No question we can get some answers that way.
>
> MARKET ANALYST: That will take too long. We already know why people eat popcorn. Our research tells us that 75% of popcorn purchases are made by males, married, ages 25 to 35. They buy it while they wait for their wives to finish shopping for other groceries. Popcorn is an impulse sale. We already know that.
>
> V-P MARKETING: Well, maybe the answer is simpler than we thought. We just have to make sure that our prime customers

buy more popcorn. When do men go shopping?

MARKET RESEARCHER: Most of them on Thursday evenings and Friday afternoons — with their wives.

DISPLAY MANAGER: Well then, the solution *is* simple. We'll just put popcorn stalls at the entrance to every main aisle in the store.

MARKET RESEARCHER: No, no. We don't have to do that. We already know that men don't hang around the soap or canned goods sections. All we have to do is put popcorn machines in the areas where men do spend their time. According to my analysis that's the cheese counter, the deli foods, the prepared-meat sections and the magazine counter.

V-P MARKETING: Good thinking, gang. Let's wheel out those machines every Thursday night and make sure they're in the right position so we can hit those impulse buyers hard.

DIRECTOR OF PACKAGING: Say, boss, how about this? Why don't we change the design of our popcorn bags? Candy-striped bags are out these days anyway. We know men react to sexy models. And every man wants to look thinner and have more hair. So we use a photo of a trim, well-muscled male model with lots of hair. He's eating popcorn and a beautiful blonde in a bikini is beside him, admiring his muscles. That should do the trick.

V-P MARKETING: Now we're really cooking, gang.

SPECIAL PROMOTIONS MANAGER: Listen up, there's something else we can do. Who can resist the smell of freshly popped popcorn? A smell like that will get an impulse buyer every time.

PURCHASING MANAGER: But how can we do that? We buy our popcorn prepackaged and it's delivered to the stores a week ahead of time.

SPECIAL PROMOTIONS MANAGER: No problem at all. We'll make it look like our popcorn has just been freshly popped. We'll heat up the bags with infrared lamps. We'll install an aroma machine above the popcorn stalls to blow synthetic, freshly made popcorn smell into the aisles. It can't fail.

V-P MARKETING: People, I think we've got it. Let's go to it. I want that 1½% back and more on top. That should make the boss happy — and it won't hurt us at bonus time either.

A flight of fantasy? Not really. Professional researchers and analysts — all the people on the marketing team — are familiar with all your habits and mine. They know exactly how to tempt us and they know that we will buy certain goods on impulse. They know where to get us, when to get us and how to get us. These are the same people who counsel cake mix manufacturers to require a fresh egg be added to the mix at home when it's really not necessary. Their research reveals the fact that most of us like the idea of adding an egg because it makes us feel the cake will be fresh and that we are making it from scratch.

All this is not really too sinister; it's merely the standard marketing process. That process is practiced by every fair-sized corporation in Canada and throughout the world. Nearly every major manufacturer has a research department or uses an outside consultant whose job is to get to know you, your habits, your weaknesses, how to sell to you and how to part you from your money. It's nearly an exact science.

Look what advertising can do, for instance. If you ever doubt the effectiveness of advertising just check out how much of their profits companies spend on it. They know it works. You can turn your nose up at any commercial you want, but it usually affects you in some way. Look at the brand labels on the clothes you are wearing or the type of car your are thinking of buying. Ask yourself if you have seen those things advertised lately.

And Where Do You Get the Money to Buy All This Stuff?

Marketing (and advertising) helps establish the demand for products and services. But you've got to have money to pay for them. If you haven't saved enough money to buy that enticing red convertible or four-by-four van, you can always use your plastic (credit card). If that isn't enough, just go to the bank or trust company and borrow what you want. It's amazingly easy to do that these days. In fact, the financial institutions work hand in hand, sometimes directly and always indirectly, with producers of our goods and services. Banks and trust companies have transformed themselves in this regard during the past few years. Today they are scrambling like mad, falling over each others' (and your) feet, to make sure you have enough money to buy the vast assortment of merchandise that is so seductively exposed to you.

Remember what banks used to be like? I think back more than a half dozen years to a time when I wanted to borrow close to $30,000 for investment purposes. I only needed it for 90 days because I knew I had a substantial bonus coming that would allow me to pay the loan off. So, I dropped into my friendly neighborhood bank to beg for a few bucks.

I quickly discovered that the amount was beyond the discretion of an assistant and I had to meet with the senior loan manager. I completed all the forms he thrust at me with all the detailed financial information they required. Then they let me stew for about a week or so. When they came back to me they said that for the amount I wanted I would have to pledge security on some of our property. This I was prepared to do, even when I found out to my amazement that what they wanted was a second mortgage. This involved using lawyers, doing title searches and registering mortgage deeds, etc. But I had no other choice. The man in the three-piece pinstriped suit at one point folded his arms, looked down his nose in my general direction and informed me that bank managers and loan officers were told never to smile and never to say yes.

You probably know how I felt because you've dealt with banks before. Usually you felt less than somebody after you'd been dissected, analyzed and (sometimes) rejected. (Who can ever forget Stephen Leacock's fictional and savagely satirical first visit to the bank to open an account?) I swore I would never borrow money from a bank again. And I haven't. I repaid the loan from my bonus within the 90 days with no comment from the bank. But they charged me interest, service charges, mortgage fees and whatever else they could. I even had to pay to have the mortgage discharged.

Things Have Changed at Your Friendly Financial Institution

In the intervening years I had never borrowed from a bank, although I admit I found it increasingly difficult not to do so. However, not long ago I dropped into the bank on the ground floor of the building where I work to deposit a check into my wife's account. The teller chatted about the bank's new V.I.P. Account and the lines of credit that could go with it. I was curious to see what was going on with the marketing of bank services, so I talked with one of the senior account executives.

Things had changed, all right. I was ushered into a private office and given a cup of coffee. A cheerful woman made a competent and interesting presentation about what banks could do for people like me. To see how far they would go, I completed an application-for-credit form toting up my assets and liabilities and left it with them. The next day the account executive phoned me to say the bank would like to extend me a line of credit for an amount of money that nearly made my eyes pop out. Furthermore, she said, they would open up a discount brokerage account for stock trading and would provide overdraft protection on a current account, plus a VISA card with a substantial credit limit. I would have personalized checks in a complimentary wallet, and if I chose to use the line of credit it would be at a very attractive rate of interest.

"What security do you need for all this," I said, "a mortgage on my life?"

"None at all," she replied, "just your signature."

Wow! The amount of credit the bank was offering in total represented nearly 3 times what I had paid for my first house. With one of their cards I could withdraw or transfer funds, with generous limitations, anywhere in Canada or throughout the world. I felt like a king. I couldn't help but recall the bank's attitude the last time I talked to them about credit, years ago.

Do they want me to use the substantial line of credit? They sure do, because that's how they make their money: on the interest I pay. Oh yes, they would like to have the interest paid, but they didn't seem to care much if I ever repaid the principal.

I was sorely tempted to go ahead with it. I kept thinking about how the extra credit would speed up the process of refurbishing our new house. Until then we'd been progressing rather slowly because of the costs involved. I knew how easy it would be to buy new furniture with the credit the bank offered. And probably my wife would have me into a couple of expensive new suits. I'm perfectly comfortable with my 8-year-old grey flannel suit, I mused. And it'll last at least another 2 or 3 years. And what would happen to our carefully constructed financial plan if I went ahead and signed on the dotted line? I concluded that it would be totally inconsistent with the professional advice I give my clients about using credit (or, more to the point, not using it).

I have a confession to make and I might as well make it now. I accepted the bank's offer. "Shame," you might say. "Why should I consider this man a reliable financial advisor if he can't follow his own advice?"

Well, I am only human. And I did want to get the house finished, for my own sake and my wife's. But I didn't fall for the bank's tempting offer without careful consideration. I justified my action on two grounds:

First, I did *not* consolidate my debts. I deliberately did not borrow relatively low-cost money from the bank and pay off the balance on our two high-interest department-store accounts. That would have been easy to do and, of course, is part of many a lender's pitch, and one made credible by many newspaper financial writers from time to time. I didn't consolidate because I knew that if we still had our department-store credit cards, because we are only human, we would soon find something in the stores we couldn't do without. Then we would have a large bank debt, and we would still be building up the department-store debt and the whole thing would spin out of control. The only way to avoid doing that would be to cut up our other credit cards and throw them away — something that you are loath to do once you have gone to the trouble of establishing credit with those institutions.

Second, I carefully worked out my cash flow to determine exactly how much debt I could handle and pay off comfortably. We had run out of ready cash for home improvements, but I had a good salary and had room to pay off a certain amount more debt without disrupting our other commitments. And above all, because I had that leeway in my cash flow, handling a bit more debt did not throw my personal financial plan into disarray.

So, although I generally do not recommend that my clients acquire many (in some cases, any) credit cards or lines of credit, I felt I was justified in doing so. But only after careful, realistic consideration and specific calculations how it would affect my financial position. The point remains, however: it's almost too easy to get money today, and that's the first step toward mismanaging your personal finances.

So how do you withstand all these enticing offers from marketers and lenders? First, recognize that even if you don't buy a new car every two years you are no less "with it" and you are no less successful than your neighbors.

Then fall back on your personal financial plan. Blame the plan for not being able to spend that extra week in Mexico next winter; don't blame yourself. You have a blueprint to financial security in your plan. Don't undermine it by succumbing to the pressures of the marketplace. Your plan gives you the little bit of extra help all of us need to withstand the subtle and constant thrust of the marketing effort, what the *Toronto Star* has called "the fine art of seduction."

8

Investing Your Savings: Divide and Conquer

Very few people are natural savers. To thrive as a saver you must first develop a program for the purpose; then you have to manage the money your program generates. In Chapter 6 I described some techniques for developing a program and for planting and nourishing the saving seeds you sow, mainly through effective budgeting. Let's turn our attention now to how you handle the financial harvest you reap, how you preserve the fruits of your budgetary labors and how you replant some of your crop for further growth.

If you are like most people I know, you've started to save suddenly, without special preparation, prompted by a fit of guilt, panic or fright because yet another financial emergency has just threatened to put you into debt. So, you start (perhaps not for the first time) building a pool of capital you call your savings.

The savings "pool" way of thinking is common to most people — just take a second to review the statistics I quoted in Chapter 6. Mind you, there is little wonder that most of us have a pool mentality. It's just another way of thinking in the short term. And basically, the pattern of our lives is geared toward short-term thinking: school tests this week; exams in two months; rent, loan and car payments every month; taxes and insurance premiums at least once a year. Our financial-management horizon seldom stretches much more than 12 months ahead, and usually less.

Managing Your Savings: Separate Them

If you want your savings to grow, you'd be better switching than fighting to maintain the short-term attitude and pattern of your life. To help you make the switch from the savings pool to the asset mentality, do this: on one piece of paper make a list of all your specific savings goals. Include everything you can think of. Then, on 3 separate pieces of paper, create 3 separate categories and divide among them all the items on your master list. For simplicity we'll call the 3 categories Short-, Medium- and Long-term Savings.

You will invest your savings in these 3 categories differently. The difference is dictated partly by the liquidity you need (when you are likely to need the funds). If you aren't going to need a downpayment for a house for 7 years, there is little point keeping the savings earmarked for the house in short-term investments (unless the return happens to be better at the moment for short- rather than medium-term investments). None of the 3 categories, incidentally, includes taking a flyer on the penny stocks of the Vancouver Stock Exchange. That's speculation, not saving or investing. Mark Twain said it best: "There are two times in a man's life when he should not speculate: when he can't afford it, and when he can."

Short-Term Savings

Short term means you'll be spending what you save in this category within a year or so. Here is a sample list of possible short-term expenditures you might save, and budget for (it's not a definitive list — you can add to it or delete from it):

Christmas gifts	summer vacation	livingroom drapes
new car	a mink coat	new suit
pearl necklace	10th wedding anniversary	chimney repairs
golf clubs	stereo system	graduation present

Since you'll be spending your short-term savings at various times within the year, you'll want to keep your money fairly liquid. Banks, credit unions or trust companies are appropriate places to keep these funds. To maximize the rate of interest you earn, even in the short term, make your deposits into a non-checking account. Shop around for the institution that pays the maximum interest. Make sure that you are getting the super bonus account — don't automatically dump your money into a standard savings account. There are many types of accounts around, all with different names. Select a savings account that pays the highest interest. That probably means a non-checking account — you can withdraw what you need when you need it in cash or cashier's check.

In our family, for example, we find it helps to keep our short-term savings goals in front of our noses if we use different bank accounts, and even different banks. Within our small family we use 6 different accounts, each for a special purpose. For instance, I have a current account at a bank near my office, for convenience. This is called a bonus checking account and it pays a fairly good rate of interest, which is related to the amount of my minimum balance. I don't write many checks, so usually service charges are waived.

Once a month I write a check to my wife for the household account. She opened that account at a bank close to our home so it's convenient for her. She also uses funds from this account to buy clothing for the children, and for herself, unless it's a major clothing expense, which we handle in a little different way. Together we have a joint savings account at a third bank. This is for major clothing expenses and also for Christmas, vacations and the like. Regularly each month we have instructed the bank to transfer a certain amount from that joint account to an account at a trust company. Those funds are used to build up medium-term savings and to make our RRSP contributions.

My son has a separate savings account at a bank of his choice. He deposits 10% of everything he earns from his summer job and casual jobs during the rest of the year, into that savings account. After the amount becomes substantial enough (at least $500) it will be transferred into long-term savings. In the meantime, he never taps this account for current spending requirements. We are trying to teach him Formula B — to save 10% of everything he earns, and the rest is his to spend or keep, whatever he wants to do with it. He keeps his spending money in a second account, and adds to it any gifts he gets. That's the account from which he will fund any major expense. If he wants a new bicycle, a stereo, a guitar, karate lessons or whatever, he uses this account.

Medium-Term Savings

Medium term means you'll probably be needing the funds in this category any time from one to about 10 years or a little more. Here are a few suggestions to help you start your own list of medium-term savings:

strategic reserve	buy cottage	house downpayment
new car	one-year sabbatical	kids' education

The first account to set up when you create your medium-term savings investment portfolio is your strategic reserve. This you will use for financial emergencies or special opportunities. You can never anticipate all the emergencies that will occur during your lifetime and any single, major emergency can decimate a budget. Also, a significant opportunity missed, because you couldn't afford it at the time, could result in a lifetime of regret.

Figure on putting away at least 3 months of after-tax income in a separate account. Some experts suggest you should squirrel away up to 6 months' income in your strategic reserve. I hesitate to recommend that much because you usually cannot get maximum interest rates for a medium-term time span. You should be able to get your hands on the cash at relatively short notice, but not as quickly as short-term funds, so liquidity is not your primary concern when you invest your money.

You want to maximize the interest so look, in normal times, to a 5-year term. One of the best moves you could make is to buy locked-in, 5-year guaranteed investment certificates (GICs). They likely will offer one of the best rates of interest, and the investment is safe with no risk involved. The only time you would consider Treasury Bills or less-than-5-year GICs would be when short-term interest rates are better than long-term ones — not the normal situation but it does happen. Then you would have to roll over these 1-year investments each year. Don't worry about the high minimum purchase that most banks require for T-Bills. You can buy smaller amounts through most stockbrokers.

The one important point here is that you should never keep your strategic reserve in a bank account paying a low interest rate.

In the meantime, if you run into a dire emergency and you haven't saved enough yet or your strategic reserve funds still are tied up for another year and a half, don't worry — you can always borrow from the bank, using your savings as collateral.

You can set up separate accounts for each of your other medium-term savings goals, or lump them into one. But generally it is better to be able to monitor the progress of each savings vehicle toward its goal. So, if you do lump them together, at least allocate on paper at home among the separate goals what you save towards each so you can see how you are doing during your quarterly reviews.

Canada Savings Bonds are a good investment for medium-term savings. You might also consider a money-market mutual fund.

But remember, if you ever have to dip into your strategic reserve, you must, over a reasonable period of time, bring that reserve back up to strength again — in addition to adding to your other short- and long-term savings accounts.

Creative, Unconventional Ways to Save for the Medium-Term

Mutual Funds. If you extend your medium-term savings horizons to about 10 years, figuring it likely will take that long before you can take a sabbatical, buy a house, the summer property, or a Florida condominium, then you can contemplate putting your savings into mutual funds. Mutual funds are not appropriate for short-term savings because usually you have to pay a front-end (sales) or a back-end (withdrawal) commission on them. You need more than a year to earn back the commission costs and show some reasonable growth. Also, a short-term slide in the market could actually reduce your savings. Over a 10 year period and longer, however, most mutual funds, especially the equity funds, have performed admirably and have produced significant growth. Depending on your preference and your own level of risk tolerance you can invest in equity (common stock) mutuals, which generally can grow the most but are burdened with the built-in risk of market fluctuations; or you can be more conservative and buy a bond mutual fund, which is less risky but also less potentially rewarding. A balanced mutual fund is somewhere between, balancing its portfolio between equities and bonds and money-market investments.

Life Insurance Savings. Another good way to provide for medium-term savings is with life insurance. A relatively recent innovation in life insurance, called Universal Life, makes this possible. With this type of policy the insurance portion of the contract is flexible and you pay separate premiums for the savings and for the insurance coverage portions. Your premiums cover just the amount of life insurance in force each year. At the same time you can make contributions beyond the life insurance premiums up to a certain maximum. These extra "premium" contributions go to the savings side of the policy. You can direct your savings into the purchase of equity shares or various types of segregated funds (insurance-company versions of mutual funds) weighted toward either equities or bonds. Or you can acquire units of money-market funds or simply buy term-savings certificates guaranteed for 1, 3, 5 or 10 years. You can make full or partial withdrawals so that you can get your savings out as you approach the dates targeted for your specific spending requirements. The advantage of saving through a Universal Life policy is that you don't have to pay income tax as your savings grow through interest or capital appreciation. You will have to pay tax when you withdraw your savings, but there are ways of minimizing this.

The government limits the total amount you are allowed to save with Universal Life. That amount is determined by a formula and if you exceed the maximum, the excess is deemed to be a savings plan rather than a Universal Life plan and is taxed accordingly. However, the maximum you are allowed is quite high and this can be an excellent way to save for the medium term.

Home Ownership. As far as saving for the downpayment on a house is concerned, the more you can put aside, and the faster, the better. The way house prices have caught fire in many parts of the country — far in excess of the rate of inflation — means that the amount you need to save for a downpayment keeps mounting with leaps and bounds rather than manageable increments. At the same time the federal government eliminated the Registered Home Ownership Savings Plan a few years ago so there is no longer any tax advantage in saving to buy a home. The Province of Ontario has introduced a plan for first-time home buyers to save tax while accumulating a downpayment. But the saving is usually less than $100 per year and it is unlikely to be of interest to most potential buyers. Albertans also can qualify for a small benefit when buying a home for the first time.

This means that you might have to look to mutual funds to produce enough savings to buy a house. Some of the more aggressive equity funds produce a return that outstrips inflation, over a period of time. But, again, there is risk involved since your savings are subject to the volatility of the stock market.

A Good Way to Save: Buy a House with No Money Down. There are a number of ways to buy a house without a downpayment. Most are complicated and too detailed to discuss here, but generally there are some investors floating around who are willing to put up the down-payment for you. You sign a long-term lease at a reasonable rental, and the investor allows you to share in the equity-growth of the house. You might have an option to buy the house from the investor in 5 years' time, with the investor taking back a second mortgage for the downpayment. The cost of the house, for instance, might be set at the original buying price plus half the increase in its value since you signed the lease. It pays to know some dependable real estate people who may be able to help you find this type of deal, especially if you are a first-time buyer. A good agent can often come up with ways of getting you a house with a lot less up-front money than you might expect.

Education Can Be on Your Medium-Term List. Educating your children is either a medium- or long-term saving proposition, depending on the amount of money needed and the ages of the children. There are a number of specific ways to save for education apart from term deposits or mutual funds, and some of them save you tax, too.

If you have children, one way is to use the family allowance check each month. Either you deposit the checks in a bank, credit union or trust company account or use them to pay the premiums of a life insurance policy, or any mutual funds. The account or the insurance or fund must be held in trust for the child. This means the interest that accumulates in the account is income, but it is taxable in the child's hands. Since the child likely will have a total income too low to be taxable, taxes will not erode or retard the growth of this special education fund.

Everything else that is invested on behalf of a child, by parents, grandparents or whatever donor, is taxable. But not family allowance.

Another similar way to save for your child's education is through a life insurance policy, so long as it is designated an "exempt" policy. In this case there is no tax payable at all on the yearly accumulation, either by the child or parent. When the child reaches age 18 the funds can be withdrawn. Then, of course, income tax is payable. But an 18-year-old probably has an income below the taxable level and won't have to pay anything.

There is a whole range of registered educational savings plans (RESP) from various financial institutions. Some of them allow you to save in small, regular payments. These include the Canadian Scholarship Trust Plan, the Heritage Trust Fund and the University Scholarship Trust Fund. You buy units of the fund on behalf of your child and you pay no income tax as the funds accumulate.

There is what you might consider a certain risk to this type of plan: if you withdraw the funds early or if your child does not go on to an appropriate post-secondary institution, you lose all the interest built up in the fund. You do get back the principal, however. The interest goes into the fund's pool to provide scholarships for those who do continue with their education. If your child does attend an accredited community college or university, the fund returns to you the principal you contributed over the years, to use for first-year fees. From then on, each year is financed, at least in part, by the fund's interest pool. The amount the funds pay each year is determined actuarially and can vary.

There are other forms of registered educational savings plans and these sometimes call for a lump sum to be deposited. This grows through interest accumulating in a tax-sheltered environment. When the funds eventually are used, they become taxable. This type of fund tends to allow more flexibility in permitting changes of designated beneficiary, and that beneficiary need not be an immediate relative. In fact, you yourself, if you are the donor, could use the funds to further your own post-secondary education. If you don't use the money for education, however, you must forego the interest your lump sum has earned, as is the case in other funds.

If you are contributing over a period of time to an educational fund, you can buy insurance to cover continued contributions. This means that if you as the donor were to die or become seriously disabled, the ongoing monthly contributions would be paid by the insurer and your child's plan would continue to grow as if you had remained alive or in good health.

This is not a comprehensive list of every savings and investment method available — new financial products, like dandelions, seem to pop up almost every day. But it does show you that there are many ways to maximize your return on savings that you won't need for a specific period of time. The main thing is to segregate your various saving needs and earmark them for specific time periods and the appropriate means of earning the best return for those periods. Don't dig a single savings pool — your hopes for financial independence will likely drown in it.

There are other excellent ways of saving, so keep an open mind. One could be some sort of thrift savings plan where you work, with automatic payroll deduction so you don't have to juggle transfers. In some cases an employer will match an employee's savings for the purchase of shares in the company. Some companies will provide assistance with post-secondary education by adding to or matching an employee's savings for that purpose. And, of course, there are rafts of scholarships available to qualifying students. Some of these are through the university itself, some are from various levels of government and some from the private sector. Don't pass up the possibility of any of these sources.

Long-Term Savings

Saving for the long term means saving probably for anywhere from 15 to 45 years. Here are a few of the categories you might need long-term savings for:

retirement	early retirement	start own business
return to school	disabled family members	for children
leave an estate		for charity

When you think of long-term savings, the natural tendency is to focus on providing retirement income. Typically most people have age 65 front and center in their minds. And although retirement at 65 or thereabouts is not the only purpose for your long-term savings program, it is undoubtedly the most important. It is important because while most people adhere to the widespread notion that their company and government pensions will see them comfortably through retirement years, it's not true in most cases. (See Chapter 10.) These pensions combined usually fall far short of what most of you need in retirement years. So, it is essential that you add a long-term, retirement component to your savings program.

If you plan to retire early and golf all winter in Florida or Hawaii, travel extensively, go back to school or start your own business as soon as you can, then more than ever you need to save for the longer term. Since we are all subject to the vagaries of the human condition, what you plan isn't necessarily what you will get. Your health might deteriorate, precluding work. You might be laid off at age 54 and unable to find a decently paying job. The only way to be prepared for almost every contingency is to save and save and save for the future. The ideal way to do this is with RRSPs. (See Chapter 9.)

Generally speaking, you should invest the money you earmark for long-term savings in equities — the common shares of companies listed on major stock markets. Equities have the best chance, based on historical performance, of growing in value substantially, and at a rate considerably more than the cost of living. That is the kind of growth you will need so you can pile up a nest-egg large enough to make you financially independent. You should be going for an average annual growth of about 15% or more from your funds. Corporations aim at 15% to 18% (or more) return on the equity they invest in their businesses. There is no reason your personal investment goals shouldn't be in the same league.

You can do this by investing in individual stocks if you are an astute stock-market trader. Or you can buy good equity-oriented mutual funds and rely on the professional fund managers to build your retirement income for you. Good equity funds can over a period of time (3 years, if you are lucky, but count on at least 10) reasonably produce at least 15% compound growth from interest and capital appreciation. This means your savings would double in value every 5 years, on average. If you use a simple investment technique known as *dollar cost averaging,* you will minimize your risk and maximize the capital gains potential of your investments. (See more about dollar cost averaging and RRSPs in Chapter 9.)

Above all, don't follow the lead of many people who place their long-term savings in short-term investments. It's a mistake. Don't keep your retirement funds in a bank account, even one with the highest bank interest: it will never approach the double-digit figures you need for maximum growth. And, of course, a bank account is outside an RRSP, so whatever it earns will be taxable. Don't buy 1-year term deposits or guaranteed interest certificates or T-Bills.

These are all shorter-term savings vehicles.

It's true that as you approach retirement you switch more and more of your equity investments to more secured or guaranteed forms of savings — you cannot always time your 65th birthday with a peak in the marketplace. Nor should you expose yourself to much risk as you get older. If you are still in equities at retirement, and the stock market is in a deep trough, as it can be in the short run, your savings could have dropped into the same trough. So a few years before retiring or planning to use your funds, start switching them to more secure types of investments.

Hands Off Pension Money

If you change jobs and gain access to the proceeds of your pension funds, keep your hands off them. Don't consider the situation a golden opportunity to grab the money and run to your nearest car dealer. That's a mistake that would have horrendous long-term consequences — if you spend $1,000 of your suddenly freed-up pension money when you are 20 years of age, it means you'll have $72,000 less to retire on at age 65.

You needn't use an RRSP for long-term growth. If you want to become financially independent by age 55 or 60 with no potential taxes payable (as there would be if you liquidated an RRSP at that time) you can still accumulate substantial sums by investing in mutual funds over a long period of time, outside an RRSP.

We have now covered how to save, how to budget and what to do with the money your savings programs generate. If you already have put that into practice, you have built the foundation of your personal financial plan. You are in the process of becoming monetarily self-sufficient and the master of your financial fate. You are moving toward that desirable state of mind epitomized by George Bernard Shaw's character in *Mrs. Warren's Profession* who said: "People are always blaming their circumstances for what they are. I don't believe in circumstances. The people who get on in the world are the people who get up and look for the circumstances they want, and, if they can't find them, make them."

9

RRSPs — The Most Misunderstood Savings Device

RRSPS. An RRSP is the single most important investment you are likely to make as part of your long-term savings program. In fact, an RRSP might well be your *entire* long-term savings program. Everybody talks about them but few people understand them. I am going to talk about them here (at the risk of boring those of you who think you really do understand them) because your RRSP is a major building-block of your financial plan.

Canada has one of the most generous retirement savings programs in the world. We are allowed to defer tax on more income than even U.S. citizens can. Their federal plan similar to our RRSP, called an IRA, is far more severely limited as to maximum contributions.

RRSPs are both a blessing and a curse. A blessing because they are undoubtedly the best way of saving for the long term since they have the potential of giving you the best growth and return for your savings. A curse because most people buy them for the wrong reasons and therefore often buy the wrong kind. When you buy the wrong kind, you won't get the return you need to pile up enough savings to keep ahead of inflation or to grow an egg large enough to hatch and feather your financial nest for later years.

Consider the 30-year-old son of a friend of mine. The young man's grandmother sent him a check to help with a downpayment for a house he was negotiating to buy. Fortunately for him he had already saved enough for his downpayment. He decided he ought to do more than dump the extra $1,000 into his bank account. Since this was in January, he was bombarded by the RRSP birds singing their seductive songs on all the radio and television stations, and awed by the legions of their ads in newspapers and magazines. On the spur of the moment one day he succumbed and dropped into his bank to ask about RRSPs. He was confronted with a bewildering batch of folders and explanations extolling the bank's various RRSP products. He soon gave up trying to wade his way through all the material, and simply asked for the RRSP that would give him the highest return. So, he bought his first RRSP, a 2-year term deposit earning about 10½% annual interest. The bank's sales person did not discuss his RRSP choice and/or his retirement objectives with him. Nor did the bank offer any explanation of the possible merits of other plans, especially the self-directed ones that might have offered him much more flexibility. Just "slam, bam, thank you, ma'am; just sign here on the dotted line," and his money was locked in for 2 years whether interest rates should slide up or rocket sky-high fast and furious, as they did in the early 1980s.

When I talked with him shortly thereafter and mentioned some of the various RRSP options, he was understandably upset with himself for not knowing and with the bank for not mentioning them. I think he is typical of many RRSP buyers, especially first-time buyers. I felt sorry for him because all the forces of the marketplace are aligned against him, urging him to jump, and jump fast, because the deadline was approaching. Even if he'd had enough time to thoroughly investigate the market (and he didn't) he would not have been sure how to go about it. He knows now he should have taken more time to learn about RRSPs, and the next time he has some spare cash he will know he should consider an RRSP investment in a time frame longer than 2 years. He has learned that there are a number of options that could bring him significantly higher returns.

What's in a Name?

RRSP — registered retirement savings plan. The very name encourages confusion and misunderstanding. The first thing you should understand about RRSPs is that they are not plans at all. An RRSP is simply permission for you, brought about by federal legislation, to register up to a certain sum of money each year in what amounts to a personal pension plan. This will allow you to supplement your income from other pension sources, if any, in later years. In your RRSP pension plan, or plans (you can have more than one), you may deposit a wide range of investments, depending on the type of plan. There are two reasons for saving this way:

1. An RRSP is a tax shelter. Your savings grow much more quickly than they would outside an RRSP because your assets in the plan are not taxed as long as the plan remains registered. Tax actually is deferred until you close the plan, and even then there are some options available that could minimize what you might have to pay Revenue Canada.
2. The contribution you are allowed to make each year, up to a legislated maximum, is deductible from that year's taxable income. This reduces your current tax load and is intended to be both an incentive to save and a way of making it more financially feasible for you to do so.

For these two reasons, RRSPs provide probably the best method of saving for your long-term financial independence.

Do You Qualify for an RRSP?

Anybody who has earned income may contribute to one or more RRSPs. Earned income is money you have received in salary or commissions or by renting property. It does not include capital gains, anything you inherit, receive as a gift or as dividends or interest. The amount of earned income you have, for RRSP purposes, is described as "total employment income" on your tax form, if you are a wage earner. If you are self-employed the amount is described as "Self-Employment Income." If you have both types of income, add them.

You can open an RRSP any time up to December 31 of the year in which you turn 71. Until that age you can make contributions to your RRSP up to 60 days beyond year-end. January and February contributions can be deducted from your taxable income from either the previous or the current year, or split between them.

Many people think that tax shelters are only for the rich — those in the top (and beyond) tax bracket. Not at all. An RRSP is *everybody's tax shelter.*

"Okay," you might be saying by now, "but a tax shelter can't make *all* that much difference."

Wrong. The difference can be staggering. If you save inside an RRSP you will end up with more than twice as much money in your long-term savings program, perhaps 3 or 4 times more than you would save outside the RRSP. Suppose you are 25 years old, in a 30% tax bracket and you start contributing $2,000 each year in an RRSP. At tax-return time each year, or shortly after, you get a tax refund of $600, so in fact your $2,000 contribution has only cost you $1,400. You make your contribution every year for 40 years, to age 65. How much do you end up with in your tax-deferred RRSP kitty? If you averaged a return of 12% per year (which is modest enough) you'd find you had piled up the resounding total of $1,718,285 — almost $1.75 million. That's almost enough to buy a box in Toronto's SkyDome! Certainly enough to fund a pretty comfortable retirement.

Now let's compare that total with the same $1,400 net, invested in a regular savings account at 12% outside an RRSP. After 40 years of saving $1,400 regularly every year, and regularly paying tax on the interest your savings earn, the total accumulation available to fund your retirement income would be only $436,973 — more than 4 times less than the same amount saved in an RRSP!

A quick look at this table will show you the different results of saving inside and outside an RRSP, in graphic terms:

TOTAL SAVED AFTER:

	10 Years	15 Years	20 Years	30 Years	40 Years
Outside RRSP	$22,407	$42,512	$72,603	$185,055	*$ 436,973*
Inside RRSP	$39,309	$83,507	$161,397	$996,926	*$1,718,285*

Note: These figures are based on a modest contribution of $1,400 net each year, earning 12% interest, and a 30% tax rate (for non-RRSP savings).

Little wonder that RRSPs have grown, and are continuing to grow, to be so popular. RRSPs have added substantially to the national wealth of the average Canadian since their introduction back in 1957. At the end of 1987 the total savings in RRSPs was close to $100 billion dollars. This sum is expected to snowball to $250 billion by 1995 — *a quarter of a trillion dollars.*

Here Is What You Can Contribute Each Year

The rules governing RRSPs change from time to time and so does the maximum amount you are allowed to contribute each year. Your maximum contribution depends on your earned income. You may contribute up to a specified dollar amount each year, but no more than a certain percentage of your earned income (based on your income of the previous year, as of 1990). As of the end of 1989, these were the maximums for those not participating in a company registered pension plan:

Tax Year	Dollar Contribution Limit	% of Earnings Limit	Earnings Needed to Make Maximum Contribution
1990	7,500	20%	37,500
1991	11,500	18%	63,900
1992	12,500	18%	69,450
1993	13,500	18%	75,000
1994	14,500	18%	80,600
1995	15,500	18%	86,100

Note: after 1995, increases in the dollar contribution limit will be indexed according to a formula.

If you are a member of a registered pension plan (RPP) or deferred profit-sharing plan (DPSP) at work, your maximum contribution limit to a personal RRSP is a bit different. In 1990 you can contribute $3500 to your own RRSP minus whatever you have contributed to your pension plan at work. From 1991 on, the maximum limits are the same as those in the table above, *but* they are reduced not only by whatever you contribute to your pension at work, the reduction must also include the amount your employer contributes on your behalf.

Since limits will be based on previous year's income, and if it is difficult to establish the amount of the employer contribution, the government will determine your allowable RRSP contribution limit and send you the figure by November.

A new wrinkle in the regulation the government has proposed will especially benefit those people whose incomes fluctuate from year to year. Starting in 1991, if you can't make a contribution in one particular year, you can "save" that unused contribution for up to seven years and then make it in a year when you are more flush — in addition to the usual contribution for that year. This means you are not penalized so much if your income drops temporarily.

Before considering the different kinds of RRSPs, let's take a look at what happens to them when you mature them.

Maturing Your RRSP — the Options

By the end of the year in which you turn 71, you must "mature" or "collapse" your RRSP. This means close it. You don't have to wait until you are 71, but you can't contribute or continue your plan later than that.

You have three options when you mature an RRSP:

- Take the money into your income.
- Buy an annuity (or annuities) with the funds.
- Start a registered retirement income fund (RRIF) with the money.

What you decide to do is critical. Once you've done it, you usually can't change it. Before you decide, there are a number of questions you have to answer about your anticipated needs. Even after you have answered those, another round of questions pops up because there is a great variety of choice both of annuities and RRIFs. If you have never done so before, this is the time to consult a qualified personal financial planner who can explain the ramifications of the choices you might be inclined to make — *before* you make them.

It would take too much space to go into detail here. Financial products keep changing, and new ones are introduced every year. It takes an expert to keep up with the marketplace and give you objective recommendations.

Taking the Money. If you cash in your RRSP, you have to take the money into income that year and pay tax on it at your full marginal rate. (Marginal means the rate you pay on your top dollar of income.)

If you have a fairly sizable plan, that will probably propel you into the top tax bracket, if you aren't there already. This option is obviously the least desirable.

If your plan is small enough, it could make sense to simply cash in the RRSP since the tax implications are not important. Or you could take a certain amount over several years, to keep the tax to a minimum. But usually it's best to forget this option.

Buying an Annuity. An annuity pays you a fixed amount of money on a regular basis for a specified period of time, or for life. Payments usually are monthly but can be set for whenever you arrange them with the company where you buy the annuity. When you buy the annuity (or annuities) with your RRSP funds, you don't pay any tax immediately. But you do pay tax on all annuity payments made to you.

The amount you'll receive each month is determined by the type of annuity and especially the prevailing interest rates at the time you buy it. If you wait until the year you are 71 before maturing your RRSP and buying an annuity, you have less flexibility in your choice because annuity income is determined in part by interest rates. If rates are low that year, your monthly income will be lower than if you had made your annuity purchase when rates were higher. The size of monthly annuity payouts is also determined by your age at the time of purchase. If you buy an annuity at age 50, your monthly checks will be lower than they would be if you were 65 or 70 because presumably you will be receiving many more of them over a longer period.

You know exactly how much you will be receiving each month and for how long when you buy an annuity. If your personality requires that kind of certainty, you might consider that an advantage. However, annuities generally don't give you much protection against inflation. You can buy one type that is indexed, but if the index rate you select is low and inflation rises above it, your standard of living will drop. Also, you have no control over how your retirement funds are invested with an annuity. That can be an advantage or not, again depending on your point of view. If you want, you can buy an annuity with survivor benefits. This means a designated survivor can continue to receive benefits from the annuity.

Buying an RRIF. Until the past few years, annuities have been by far the most popular way to mature a RRSP. However, RRIFs are gaining fast because they are more flexible and over a long period of time may pay you considerably more. Some retirees choose a mix of annuities and RRIFs.

A RRIF also provides periodic payments from the time you buy it until age 90. At that point all the funds in a RRIF must have been paid out to the holder. This is done according to a government formula that specifies a certain minimum percentage of the RRIF's assets (principal) must be paid to you as income each year. These payments tend to be small for the first few years, if you take the minimum allowable, and larger as you become older. You can, of course, withdraw more than the minimum at any time for whatever purpose if you haven't bought a RRIF that locks your investments in (such as a 5-year GIC). Hence, RRIFs tend to be the most flexible RRSP maturity option. If you don't need a high payment in the few years following your purchase, your RRIF assets usually continue to grow for some years, because, like RRSPs, there is no tax payable on funds still in the RRIF, only on what you take out each year. Therefore the total payout over time tends to be much larger than the total payout of an annuity.

Other advantages include:

- You can leave your RRIF, like an RRSP, to your spouse or other beneficiary if you die before the funds are exhausted. Your spouse can defer taxes longer by rolling the remaining assets over into a new RRIF in his or her name, but the assets become taxable in the hands of any other beneficiary.
- You have a degree of control over the way your RRIF funds are invested. RRIFs are like RRSPs in that you can buy certain kinds of plans that suit your circumstances, including potentially higher-yield equities or equity mutual funds. A RRIF can be a single investment, or can, like a self-directed RRSP, be flexible, containing several different types of investments that you can change according to your needs.
- You can start a RRIF at any age.
- You have a degree of inflation protection if you don't take huge payouts at the start, and you can place high-yield investments in your RRIF.

When you opt for either RRIFs or annuities, the payments you receive are considered pension income, and after age 65 you can receive a tax credit each year on the first $1,000 of pension income. So, even after you have liquidated your RRSP, you still get a tax break.

Not All RRSPs Are the Same

You can group the huge variety of RRSPs available into several general categories, and none of them would produce Plutarch's "similarity of results." Nor do the individual RRSP products within each group produce equally well — some are better managed than others. Also, some plans are designed to be safe and secure and some plans embody a degree of risk but fulfill your urge (or need) to speculate. At the safe end of the spectrum are RRSPs that are nothing much more than bank or trust company savings accounts registered under RRSP legislation. At the riskier end are those containing various stock-market investments. Generally speaking, you might expect that the more secure the plan, the lower the potential return; the riskier the investment, the higher the potential. Of course, "risky" and "secure" are relative terms.

Most RRSPs are one-product plans. If you want a GIC from a bank offering a good interest rate, you open an RRSP there containing a GIC. A week later you spot a trust company advertising an even higher rate for their RRSP, so you open another one at the trust company using their single product. Sometimes a financial institution has more than one RRSP-eligible product you want, and you might be able to pop them into the same plan. But in most cases only the self-directed style of RRSP allows you to place a variety of different investments into a single plan.

You can have as many RRSPs as you wish. Since you usually have to pay an annual administration fee in each, albeit a small one, it doesn't make much sense to have a lot of different plans. You often can transfer funds from one RRSP to another, thereby minimizing the number of plans you have. But if you want variety, perhaps a self-directed plan into which you can drop almost every type of investment possible, is the one for you.

These are the eight general categories of RRSPs available:

1. Simple savings
2. Guaranteed Investment Certificates (term deposit)
3. Mutual funds
4. Life insurance savings products
5. Self-directed
6. Spousal
7. Locked-in
8. Group

1. Savings RRSPs. This is like a bank account except the interest is not taxed and therefore your savings compound more quickly. The advantage is safety: if your financial institution is a member of the Canadian Deposit Insurance Corporation (CIDC) — and most banks, trust and loan companies are — deposits are protected up to $60,000 per person per institution.

This kind of plan is liquid too — usually you can make withdrawals at any time, though doing so negates the basic premise of long-term RRSP saving. The disadvantage of this type of plan tends to be lower returns than most other plans offer. But a savings RRSP is not a bad idea as an interim measure. If you don't have time to thoroughly examine all the RRSP alternatives but want to get started immediately, it's a way to get that start. You can always transfer to another plan later.

2. Guaranteed Investment Certificates. Known as GICs for short, these certificates and/or term deposits can be registered as RRSPs. Since these plans are sold by trust companies and banks, they have the advantage of CIDC protection insurance. And the interest rates tend to be higher than simple savings plans.

You lose liquidity, however, although this may not concern you. GICs are locked in for a specific length of time extending anywhere from a few months to 5 years. The longer the period you choose, the higher the rate of interest, usually. You can buy a redeemable GIC or term deposit, but if you redeem it before its term, you probably will receive lower interest as a penalty.

When deciding which GIC or term deposit to buy as an RRSP, determine how the bank handles the interest paid. Sometimes the interest is automatically reinvested at the same rate you are getting for the GIC. Sometimes, however, the interest earns at a lesser savings-account rate.

3. Mutual Funds. You can open an RRSP based entirely on eligible mutual funds. Some funds are not eligible because their percentage of non-Canadian investments is too high. Make sure you check eligibility before you buy. Mutual funds have become popular for RRSPs if for no other reason than they offer variety: from money-market funds to common stock (equity) funds, and a combination of both.

Mutual funds are grouped into three broad categories: fixed-income funds, equity funds and balanced funds. The *income funds* usually have a portfolio mix of bonds, money-market instruments, mortgages or other income-producing investments. Some specialize in bonds or money-market investments alone. *Equity funds* are heavily weighted toward shares of publicly traded companies. *Balanced funds* combine the features of both the other types.

You can also buy specialized funds — funds that invest only in shares of specific industry groupings, or, for instance, in "environmentally acceptable" companies.

Fund managers buy and sell and change their portfolios to suit their interpretation of market conditions. Some managers will keep more cash on hand if they think the market may drop. Then they hope to be in a good position to take advantage of any good opportunities to buy. Funds tend to be advertised and sold on the basis of their managers' performances, going back a decade or more. Of course their past performance does not necessarily guarantee their future success as investors of your money. But it is the only measuring stick we have unless you buy on hunches.

Consumers buying mutual funds sometimes consider it an advantage to be able to place their money in the hands of these professional fund managers. Then, theoretically at least, you don't have to be constantly worried about buying and selling decisions, which you probably are not adequately qualified to make anyway. Let the managers do it.

You pay for this expertise. It varies from fund to fund but it can be as much as 2.5% of your assets in the fund. In addition, most funds charge a sales commission (called a "front-end load") or a withdrawal commission (called a "back-end load"). If you buy from a financial institution that offers a group or "family" of funds, you sometimes can switch from one fund to another in the family at little or no cost when you want to alter your investment strategy.

You can buy mutual-fund RRSPs directly from some fund companies themselves, from banks, trust or life insurance companies, from investment counselors and from financial planning organizations (like Money Concepts).

4. Life Insurance Savings Products. Life insurance companies sell two main types of RRSPs: fixed-income (guaranteed-interest) investments and segregated (pooled) funds. The fixed-interest plans operate much like GIC or term-deposit RRSPs. Segregated funds are similar to mutual funds and they are worth looking at because some of these have shown greater returns for the past few years than the traditional mutual funds.

Insurance-company RRSP products differ a bit from non-insurance products, though in practice they differ more in semantics than in substance. Your contract will refer to a deferred annuity, whereby the company promises to make regular payments to you starting some specified time in the future, usually 10 years or more hence. However — and many RRSP buyers consider this an advantage — your money is not locked in and you can cash in at any time and transfer your money to other RRSPs if you wish. In some cases you might have to pay a small penalty to withdraw early; sometimes not. This goes for both fixed-income and segregated (mutual) fund insurance products.

Another advantage to the life insurance funds is that, should you name any immediate family members as beneficiaries, your fund assets are protected under the Uniform Life Insurance Act and therefore cannot be seized as payment for debt. You do not have that protection with any other RRSPs.

In the case of segregated funds, some companies also guarantee to repay at least 75%, and in some cases 100% of your original contributions at maturity or at your death. If a slumping stock market at that moment happens to have slashed the value of your units, at least your estate would not be totally wiped out. This type of guarantee is also unique to insurance-company funds.

5. Self-Directed. If you want more control over your RRSP investments; if you have trouble keeping track of the various RRSPs you already have at different institutions; and if you want a variety of different kinds of investments in your RRSP, then a self-directed plan is probably for you.

A self-directed plan offers you the greatest RRSP flexibility, yet it is not complex to manage. You can plan your own investment strategy and most of the paperwork is handled by the financial institution administering your plan. You pay an annual administration fee of around $100.

You can open a self-directed plan through most investment dealers, banks and trust companies. Your financial planner can arrange it for you if you want. You then can buy and sell stocks and bonds, mutual funds and place GICs and Canada Savings Bonds in it as you choose.

You can contribute to your self-directed RRSP in cash or in eligible investments you already own, such as individual stocks and bonds, or mutual funds. When you want to buy a certain investment you instruct the plan administrator to do so, using cash in the plan. If there is not enough cash, you can sell one of the plan's investments and use the proceeds from that. You can even hold your own mortgage in your plan, if there is enough money in the plan to handle it.

"Decisions, decisions," you are probably thinking right now. "I would have to be making decisions all the time."

This is true, but if you look at an RRSP as a long-term savings method — the way you should be looking at it — you will be holding most of your investments for long periods and many decisions need only be made once — the first time. Besides, with the help of this book, and possibly a financial planner, you should be able to develop a top-notch personal financial plan, and that plan usually will guide you through most of the investment decisions you might have to make. And you can also ask your financial planner or advisor to participate in the decision-making process. Remember you are not alone; help is always available.

Not absolutely every kind of investment qualifies for a self-directed RRSP. Here is a list to help guide you:

You can put these in your self-directed RRSP:

Cash (Canadian only)

GICs, term deposits

Bonds (of the three levels of government; Canada and Quebec savings bonds, bonds, debentures, notes of corporations listed on any prescribed Canadian stock exchange *(Toronto, Montreal, Vancouver, Alberta, Winnipeg)*

Annuities issued by Canadian financial institutions

Mortgages: your property or another's, in Canada

Mortgage-backed securities; shares in most mortgage-investment companies

Call options, rights and warrants listed on a Canadian stock exchange, if they can be used to buy a qualified investment

Common and preferred shares of Canadian companies listed on a Canadian exchange (see above)

Shares of many privately held Canadian corporations. The company must be active in Canada. You cannot hold more than 10% of the company's shares in your RRSP

Units or shares of eligible mutual, closed-end or insurance company segregated (or pooled) funds
Most shares of limited partnerships, but no more than 50% of the market value of your plan
Foreign securities listed on foreign stock markets prescribed by Revenue Canada (up to 10% of your plan's value)
A share or an interest in a credit union
A share or deposit with a SODEQ in Quebec
Debt securities of widely held co-operatives

You cannot put these in your self-directed RRSP:
Foreign currency
Commodity futures or commodities
Real estate
Gold, silver, platinum, precious metals, coins
Delisted stocks (ones that are not trading)
Works of art, antiques, jewelry, gemstones

6. Spousal. This is one of the few remaining ways to split income for the purpose of reducing tax — in this case, usually at retirement time. The spousal plan can take the form of any of the preceding plans, including self-directed. You can open one and make contributions to the spousal plan up to your own legal limit. Your taxable income is reduced by the amount of the contribution, as usual, but it does not affect your spouse's contribution limit if he or she should have an RRSP also.

There are some tax ramifications if you take funds out of the spousal plan within 3 years of contributing. And when you reach age 71 and have to close your RRSPs, you can still make contributions to a spousal plan until your spouse reaches that age as well.

The idea behind a spousal plan is that you and your spouse split retirement income between you so that each pays tax at a lower rate than if all the income were to be in the hands of only one of you. Of course, remaining married is a prerequisite if you are to benefit from this maneuver.

7. Locked-in. Opening a locked-in RRSP is one of the three options available to you if you leave a company where you had a pension plan. You could leave your pension entitlements with the company, to be collected when you retire. Or you could transfer the pension to your new employer, if the new employer agrees. Or you could roll the pension into a locked-in RRSP. This type of plan is restrictive: you cannot close it or withdraw funds from it until you retire. At that time you must buy an annuity with the proceeds. However, you do have some say about the type of investments held by the RRSP, not unlike a self-directed plan.

8. Group. Your company might sponsor a group RRSP. Perhaps it might even make contributions on your behalf, making it a type of informal pension plan. There are two advantages to a group RRSP, regardless of whether your employer contributes to it. First, your contributions usually are made through automatic payroll deduction each month. This is a relatively painless way of saving, and after a while you won't even miss the lower take-home pay. Also this saves you the hassle of doing it yourself. Second, you can file a notification with Revenue Canada through your employer that your income is being reduced by the monthly contributions. This means the tax deducted from your paycheck each month will also be reduced and, in essence, you will get your tax break throughout the year instead of having to wait for it until after you file your year-end return.

You get another break, too. When you make monthly contributions throughout the year, your plan earns more income than when you make a single contribution at the end of the year.

Employers benefit as well: it is less complicated and less costly for them to administer a group RRSP than a pension plan. Almost all types of investments can be placed into a group RRSP, with the exception of individual company-equity stocks.

Five Distorted Views of RRSPs

1. The Myopic View. Every January and February in newspapers and magazines, on TV and radio, and in banks and other financial institutions, advertisements for RRSPs spring up like crocuses through the snow. There is so much hype about them in the media and by personal-finance, self-help columnists that the information tends to confuse rather than clarify the issue. Confusion occurs because the companies marketing RRSPs tend to focus their appeals to buyers on the short- rather than long-term RRSP benefits. The ad managers are shrewd and fully aware of their potential clients' short-sighted tendency to look no farther than the next few months.

It's hard not to be affected (or infected) by this view. Perhaps you are one of those who dwell mainly on the tax relief you will get a few months hence when you think "RRSP". You certainly are encouraged to think this way. So, you rush out with your money at the last minute and shove it into the most convenient vehicle you find. That vehicle is usually a money-market account, or a trust company's 1- or 2-year GIC, or perhaps even a 6-month term deposit in a bank.

If you do this, you totally disregard the intrinsic long-term, saving-for-financial-freedom nature of RRSPs. Because of your financial myopia you will never see the kind of growth you need in your RRSP that will allow you to retire with dignity at 65 or earlier. When you make a short-term investment in your RRSP you are shortchanging your own financial future. As I mentioned in Chapter 8, you should expect an RRSP return in the high teens, not 7 to 11 percentage points lower.

If you weren't getting a current-year tax break from your RRSP contribution, you'd probably be much more careful about how you chose to invest it. A good investment is a good investment only if it brings you a good return, not because it gets a tax break this year. Why lose out by concentrating on the tax implications and not the quality of the investment? Check back to Chapter 8 for some suggestions of the appropriate type of investment that will maximize your return over a long period of time.

2. The Late View. The government tells us that we can make this year's contribution to our RRSPs up to 60 days into the next year — typically March 1 (except for leap year). Because we are told that this is the last possible date to do so, our normal human trait is to wait for the end of February to make our contribution or start a new RRSP.

It's a crazy thing to do, of course. If we really understood RRSPs and the miracle of compound interest, we'd buy them at the earliest possible date, which is January 1 of the tax year concerned, 14 months earlier than most of us act. If you are typical, you're really doing yourself severe injury by waiting so long. You are missing 14 months of capital appreciation and/or interest accumulation. What that means in terms of lost asset (and income) growth after, say, 30 years, is startling. As an item in *The Financial Post* points out, if you made a contribution of only $2,000 to your plan every year at the *start* of each tax year, and earned 10% on it, you'd end up with $975,704 after 40 years. That is *$90,519 more* than if you waited to make the contributions 14 months later, at the deadline. Imagine what the gain would be if you got 12% or even 15% or 18% return in your plan. For example, after 40 years at 15% you'd have a whopping $4,091,908 — that's about *$533,000 more* because you contributed early. That translates into a yearly increase of more than $53,000 in income, assuming you can get a modest interest on the funds of just 10%.

3. The Liquid View. This is really a short-term view. Because you don't focus your RRSP thinking on the future, you continually expect you might have to get at the money you've saved in your plan. So, you put your RRSP investment or contribution into very short-term, liquid investments. For example, you might stash it in a simple savings RRSP, or 6-month GIC. You'll be able to get at your funds when you need them, sure. You'll earn perhaps 6% to 8%, maybe even 9% when interest rates are high. But you'll never see the 15% or so you need to keep ahead of inflation. That kind of return you'll only find in equities or equity-oriented mutual funds.

If you think you might need to use some of your savings in the near future, build up the strategic reserve I mentioned in Chapter 8 before you start an RRSP. The savings in the reserve should cover your short- to medium-term needs. Reserve your RRSP for the long term.

4. The Savings Pool View. This is another short-term view. You consider RRSPs just another drop in your pool of savings. If you have the pool mentality, you are likely to dip into it when you feel like it. You must switch to the asset mentality when you look at RRSPs. You use your RRSP assets to build on, and with, so the level rises over the long term, never drops.

5. The Debtor's View. Because it is the "in" thing to do, you start or contribute to an RRSP even when you can't afford to. That is the debtor's view. You don't have the $500 or $1,000 to contribute, so you join the lineup at the bank or trust company, and borrow the money. You try to pay off the loan over the next couple of years but you're frequently in arrears because you really couldn't afford to borrow in the first place. And you are not saving much in current tax because of the low amount involved.

At the same time you are not maximizing your RRSP investment because it is likely a plan offering relatively low return from the institution you borrowed from. You can't switch to a high-yield plan from another institution once you see the error of your ways because you are probably locked into the company that is lending you the money.

Does It Pay to Go Into Debt to Make Your RRSP Contribution?

Borrowing to make an RRSP contribution can be a sensible move, then, only under special circumstances. Assess your position carefully and allow yourself time to shop around for the loan and the type of RRSP before you commit yourself and the money.

Some years ago borrowing was a fairly attractive strategy in order to make your annual RRSP contribution because you could deduct the interest costs of your loan from your taxable income. Now you can't deduct such interest, but you still can benefit by doing so if you handle it properly.

First, you must be able to afford the loan payments — principal and interest — with no difficulty. Second, you should be able to pay off your loan within a year. If you can't pay it off within that time, don't borrow. You'll send yourself into an upward spiral of debt that could spin you right into bankruptcy.

This is how it works: assume your income allows you to make a contribution of $4,000 this year. You borrow the $4,000 at a fixed rate of 15%, which is compounded yearly. Your monthly interest and principal payments (based on paying off the loan in 1 year or less) are $312.40. You are in a 40% tax bracket, so your $4,000 contribution qualifies you for a tax rebate of $1,600 dollars. You use the rebate to pay down your loan principal (say, for sake of argument, 3 months after you first take out the loan). You maintain the same monthly payments, which means the loan is paid off after about 8 months. Over this period you have paid $204 in loan interest out of your pocket.

In the meantime your $4,000 contribution is earning interest in the RRSP at, say, 11%, and this builds up in a tax-deferred environment for the year. That amounts to $440 for the year. So, at the end of the year you have earned $236 (pre-tax) in interest more than you have paid out, your loan is completely paid off and your $4,000 plus the $440 interest will continue to grow, tax-free, for many years until you mature the RRSP.

This borrowing scenario works. Most others don't. Approach the idea with caution.

The RRSP/Equity Controversy

A discussion of RRSPs would not be complete without reference to the disparate views among financial "experts" on whether you should have equities or equity-based mutual funds in your RRSP. To many people, equities represent risk, and they feel that risk has no place in a retirement plan — only fixed-interest investments (like GICs or Treasury Bills) should be considered for RRSPs because they are safe. Not all financial experts or planners agree. You could sum up the two main, opposing viewpoints thus:

- RRSPs should contain only interest-bearing instruments because safety of capital is paramount, and equities (or equity-based mutual funds) lose the capital gains, capital loss and dividend income tax breaks when put in RRSPs.
- Equities do belong in RRSPs because they are the proven way to get the growth a retirement fund needs, and are the best way to beat inflation. However, the equity portion should be balanced with fixed-income vehicles.

Some financial advisors are more extreme in defense of equities and suggest that they are all you need in an RRSP.

I am one of those who believe strongly that equities must play a part in your RRSP, but how much and when depends on many factors. This is one of those questions you might seek to answer with the help of counsel from a financial advisor you trust. Here is why I believe in equities:

If you plan for the long term (the basic purpose of an RRSP), you are trying to build up as much retirement income as possible. One of the very best ways to do this is to own equities. By that I mean participating in the ownership of corporations by buying their common shares. You can buy shares in individual companies directly from the stock market through a broker. Or you can buy equity-based mutual funds — a fund that pools investor money and buys equity stocks in a variety of companies. If you are consistent in your investment strategy and do not panic and sell your equities for a loss every time the stock market drops, you will build a much bigger RRSP portfolio than you could with any other kind of investment. Every study of major stock markets ever done shows that stocks outperformed bonds and other fixed-interest investments over a 20-year period. So, if you hang in there, you'll come out ahead, especially ahead of inflation, which is the most important factor. It is the after-inflation, or "real," return you will end up with when you turn your RRSP into retirement income.

If you are within a few years of retirement, you definitely must protect your capital and reduce risk. So, you will likely move away from equities in your RRSP to more secure, interest-bearing investments. If you are younger and will not need your RRSP funds for at least 20 or more years, you are in a better position to accept the built-in risk of the equities market. At the very least you will have time to recover from any market setbacks during that period.

Risk — It's Almost Un-Canadian

Most people are frightened to death of equity or common stocks. When you realize that common stock is one of the few investments that can appreciate well beyond the rate of inflation and certainly beyond current interest rates, you might want to re-examine your attitude. As some equity mutual funds have performed at so high a return as 15% or better per year, you probably think that there must be a terrible risk involved. Well, there are risks, but not terrible ones. The key to success is not in avoiding them; it's how you handle them. A certain amount of risk accompanies every daily activity, but that doesn't mean you refuse to cross the street to go shopping. When you do cross, you are careful.

Why should you as an individual be prepared to take less risk (and less return) than a company? Almost any type of company or corporation expects, or at least works toward, a return of 18% or better on the capital invested in the company. It's neither a sin nor unrealistic for you to expect and work for a similar return from your RRSP.

The stock-market crash of October 1987 was a classic example of how many investors mismanage risk. It's interesting to note that 85% of the mutual funds that were redeemed (sold or cashed in) after the October Crash were owned by investors who had bought their funds during the 2 years preceding Black Monday. These investors bought into a market that was high after 5 years of steady growth before the

Crash, and when the market dropped dramatically, they panicked and sold out at substantial losses. For at least 1½ years after the Crash most average investors continued to shy away from equities. But you must be persistent to win with equities. Smart investors had either got out of the market before Black Monday and then went back into it immediately afterward at bargain-basement prices, or stayed with the market, even adding to their equity holdings at the low prices. They were rewarded in a shorter time than usual, because within 15 or 16 months of the Crash the market had recovered the approximately 20% it had lost.

Dollar Cost Averaging Reduces Your Risk

You can't eliminate all risk if you are in the equities market, but you can manage it so you come out ahead in the long term. If you feel helpless in predicting the swelling and ebbing of the oceans of common stocks on the market, join the crowd. Not many individual investors (or even the majority of institutional ones) always buy at the top and sell at the bottom. Be a persistent, long-term investor instead, and practice dollar cost averaging (DCA) to offset stock-market risk. The idea is to invest a fixed sum every month in equity stocks or mutual funds. If the market goes down, your fixed sum will buy more shares (or mutual fund units) the next month because the individual unit price has dropped lower. You keep this up consistently, even in a declining market. When the market does start to rise, you will have a lot more shares or units rising with it than you would have had if you'd bought them all at once for the same, higher price. You want to spend a fixed sum each month, not to buy the same number of shares or units each month.

Here's an example:

Mutual Fund A costs $10 per unit in January. You buy 10 units for $100. By February, the unit cost has dropped to $5. You could buy another 10 units for a total of $50, which would give you a total cost of $150 for the 20 shares, or an average of $7.50 each. But instead, you buy another $100 worth (or 20 units). You have now bought 30 units altogether for a total of $200, or an average cost of $6.67 per unit. So, your average cost has dropped from $7.50 to $6.67 and you have 30 units rather than 20. When the market starts to rise, you have 30 units at a lower unit cost rising with it. Usually a market will decline over a period of months (sometimes years), and during that time you will accumulate a huge number of units that will inflate your total investment with breakneck speed when the market finally turns around.

This technique works better with mutual or segregated funds than it does with individual company shares. Usually you have to buy individual shares on the stock market in standard board lots, sometimes of 50 shares, but generally in multiples of 100. You can, however, buy any reasonable number of most mutual-fund units and partial units so you can stick to your flat $100, or $1,000 purchase each month. Don't forget to keep buying as your fund increases in price as well. You can't lose in a rising market. Of course, whatever the swings of the market, the losses and gains you watch are are on paper only, until you decide to sell.

If you use DCA in conjunction with well-established funds that have a good growth record over time, or with reputable fund managers who have a good record with other funds, your RRSP will swell at the seams and you'll have enough to put away to retire with dignity, perhaps even earlier than you planned to. Again, try for a return at least of 15% per year.

A tip about mutual funds as stated earlier in the chapter: buy the fund manager, not the fund. The manager or managers make it go, and if they move elsewhere, the fund may not perform as well. A manager's record really is the only measurable information you have.

You Can Never Outsmart the Tax Department

Don't ever think that by using RRSPs you are going to outfox the tax department. Many financial experts and manuals written about RRSPs advise their clients and readers to roll over their RRSP and RRIF assets continuously in an attempt to defer taxes, so you can leave a tidy estate for your kids. Forget it. You can't. You can pass on your RRSP or RRIF to your spouse when you die and he or she can roll it over into a personal plan, deferring taxes a while longer. But if you die single or when your surviving spouse eventually dies, your RRSP or RRIF immediately becomes income in your estate.

The tax department has been patient and this is where it eventually gets its pound of flesh. In fact, it might get two pounds. While the estate's marginal tax rate might normally be around 30%, an RRSP of any reasonable size added in could easily shoot it swiftly into the 50% tax-rate range. So, the RRSP could be cut in half before any beneficiary sees it. It's hard to win when the government wants your money, as we saw in Michael Wilson's budget in spring 1989.

The moral is, don't fuss too much about taking some of your RRSP or RRIF assets into income from time to time as you get older. Use the money to enjoy yourself. As the cliches have it, you're only here once, and you can't take it with you. Equally true, you can't even pass all of it along.

This has been by no means a definitive discussion of RRSPs — it's more a basic introduction. With so many types of RRSPs, so many products you can put in them and so much hype about them (to say nothing of tax implications) you would be wise to seek some objective advice if you are approaching them for the first time. Or if you want to change your strategy. You are likely to get the best advice from a financial planner who has access to most of the products on the market and has no special ax to grind in suggesting one to you over another.

Also the government changes RRSP regulations faster than you can blink an eye and more often than a snake sheds its skin. Keep your eyes peeled when reading the business pages so you don't miss news of pertinent legislation or a rule change. Using a planner is also a good way to keep in touch with RRSP and all legislation that bears on money management and financial planning.

10

Job Security – A Myth

Do you have a cozy dream that after retirement you'll be living on Easy Street thanks to your company and government pensions? If you do, you're in for a rude awakening. Do you think you'll be with your company for years and that you'll have loads of time to build up pension and savings assets? Think again. For most Canadians, working 9 to 5 is not what it used to be, and visions of a carefree financial future flowing entirely from a secure job and pension, plus government Old Age Security and Canada Pension Plan (CPP) payments, is sheer myth. Unless you are, that is, a government employee or possibly a teacher with a fully indexed pension.

Most of you reading this book, however, had better learn, as I did, to depend *only* upon yourselves if financial freedom is your goal. You'll attain that goal only if you, and you alone, develop the discipline to save systematically and build up your assets. Then, in later years, you can convert those assets to income when you need it.

The simple fact is that you'll have to rely on yourself because the combined income from your company pension plan, CPP and Old Age Security payments will not be nearly enough to support a comfortable life in retirement anywhere close to the level you experienced when working. If you're self-employed, work part time or have no employment income, you are already aware of this grim fact of life.

Most of Us Don't Have Private Plans

If you were to judge solely from the amount of time and space the media give news about union activities, you'd think that most Canadians were well covered as far as pension plans are concerned. This is far from the case. Only about 40% of our working population is covered by pension schemes. The remaining 60% work either for medium-sized companies that may offer a few benefits but no pension, or for the approximately 775,000 small businesses in Canada that are purported to generate the majority of our country's jobs. These small operations more often than not extend absolutely no beyond-salary benefits of any kind — pensions included — to their employees. Most self-employed people don't have pensions either.

Pension legislation comes under the jurisdiction of the provinces but what the more populous provinces do tends to set the trend as all provinces try to standardize regulations across the country. In Ontario, for example, pension plans are not mandatory in firms with fewer than 15 employees, and if the company doesn't want to offer a plan, there is none. And with larger companies the mandatory requirements for pensions in a province even the size of Ontario are minimal.

Only recently Ontario set what is expected to be a trend by reducing the waiting time until an employee's pension is vested. (Vesting is the right to acquire title to the pension contributions made by the employer on your behalf.) And the new laws insist that the shorter vesting period applies only to contributions made from the time the new law was enacted. So, all previous contributions are not necessarily vested until a certain number of years after you join a plan. The number of years was determined by the employer and could be as many as 10. If you leave your job before your pension is vested, you get from the plan only what you yourself have put into it, plus some interest, whether you transfer it to a new employer's plan, or simply take the money in cash. If only your employer had made contributions, you get nothing. If you are a young employee and expect to have at least 10 different jobs in your lifetime, you'd better pay attention to how your pension is vested or you could end up with little or none of it at all.

If You Get It, Don't Spend It

When you leave a company for another job, you sometimes gain access to your pension savings. If you do, you could be terribly tempted to take your pension funds in cash and spend them on a new sofa or red convertible. Don't. Resist that temptation and consider the opportunity you have that many others don't. If you get your hands on a lump of cash in that way, instead of spending it, start or add to a RRSP. If your new employer will accept the transfer of your previous pension contributions, perhaps do that. Do almost anything. But don't spend it.

Pension Benefits Are Becoming Less Well Defined

The trend toward money-purchase pension plans in corporations rather than defined-benefit plans is further evidence that you'd better depend on your own resources and not on the company pension. A defined-benefit plan defines, in advance, the amount of pension income you will get when you retire. The calculation is based on a formula that varies from plan to plan and that averages 5 or so of your highest-income years, usually the last 5 years on the job. It is designed to pay out an annual benefit of about 70% of that average. So, you know in advance that you can plan on a certain sum in the future. If the plan's investments don't pan out too well and its earnings are not enough to pay the defined amount at retirement, the employer is obliged to make up the difference — if it can afford to. On the other hand, if the plan's investments exceed expectations, the employer usually takes over any surplus produced, not the employee. A paternalistic employer might use a surplus to increase the defined payout, but it is not obliged to do so.

The income you'd receive from a money-purchase pension plan, however, depends strictly on how well the investments bought by the plan manager perform. If they do well, you'll get more. If they don't, you'll get less when you retire. In any event, you won't really know how much you'll get until you get it. That makes personal financial planning rather difficult.

For a number of reasons, including the fact that they are less complicated and less expensive to manage, employers are shifting quickly toward money-purchase plans. This is true especially in Ontario where the law now specifies that defined-benefit pensions in the private sector must be partially indexed each year. This will add to the employer's cost. About 80% of all pension plans in Canada have traditionally been of the defined-benefit type. But the number of money-purchase plans is growing fast and in 1988 they accounted for 14% of all plans, compared to only 5% 2 years previously.

Company Pensions Are Not Necessarily What They Seem

Even if you have a company pension, do you really know what that means in terms of total retirement income? How long has it been since you took a careful look at your pension-plan formula and the income you expect from it compared to your future needs? When you do you may be shocked.

As I mentioned, defined-benefit pension plans calculate your projected retirement income according to a formula. That formula often offsets what you'll get from the government. A typical working person with 15 years or so of service and contributions to a company plan, can, in reality, expect to receive a yearly pension income at retirement of about 52% of his or her final year's income before retirement. That means a drop in income of about 48%. How many people can afford that? If *you* can't, you'll have to make up the difference from your own personal retirement program. Better start planning for that eventuality right now.

To illustrate this critical point, imagine the kind of scenario that happens every day at various corporations across the country. (You might be a long time from retirement, but there is no reason to think that this scenario won't still be valid when you decide to call it a day.) The *Old Timer* (OT) is six weeks from retirement and he's been called up to the personnel office for a pension-benefits review with a personnel consultant (PERCON) and to make some critical decisions. A typical session might go something like this:

> OLD TIMER: Well, it's only 6 weeks away. I'm really looking forward to that first big pension check after 35 years in this sweat shop.
>
> PERCON: That's right, Old Timer. And you deserve to be able to relax after all that time. Today we have to make some decisions so we can put everything to bed and be ready for 6 weeks from now.

OT: Well, first of all I'd like to make sure that my pension checks come in every 2 weeks and that you send them down to Florida when I'm there during the winter. Yes, sir, that $35,000 a year is going to come in handy.

PERCON: Well now, not quite $35,000, Old Timer. How did you arrive at that figure?

OT: Well, 35 years on the job at 2% per year. That's 70%. I'm pulling down $50,000 a year. That's pretty simple mathematics and it works out to $35,000 a year.

PERCON: Perhaps we should look a little more closely at the pension formula. It calls for the average of your last 5 years of service prior to retirement.

OT: So, what difference does that make?

PERCON: Well, your salary 5 years ago was $40,000, right? It went up gradually every year to your current $50,000, that's true. But the average of those 5 years is $45,000. When we take 70% of $45,000, it comes to $31,500 a year, not $35,000.

OT: Holy smokes, I guess you're right. I've never looked at the details before. It looks like I'm going to have to study this pretty closely over the next 6 weeks. Anyway my Canada Pension Plan and Old Age Security checks should bring it back to around $35,000.

PERCON: Oh not really, Old Timer. You see, the company's pension plan, like many others, is blended in with the Canada Pension Plan and Old Age Security, so you don't get those over and above your $31,500.

OT: Here and I thought I was going to be getting $70% of final earnings plus all these government benefits, and now you're telling me that I'm only gong to get about 63%? Period?

PERCON: That's right. Of course you'll get that amount as long as you live and even your wife would get it for the 10 years after you retire in case you don't live that long. You do want to make sure that there's some money for your widow in case you die during the next 10 years?

OT: Well, I'd certainly want Martha to get that $31,500 if I die. That's what pension means, doesn't it? I get it as long as I live and then she gets it when I die, as long as she lives?

PERCON: No, that's not exactly right. The terms of the pension plan are listed as "10 years certain." That means you certainly get it for the rest of your life. By the way, how old is Martha?

OT: 62.

PERCON: You get your pension for the rest of your life. But, if you die, Martha would be assured of an income until she's 72. Does she work, and does she have Canada Pension Plan?

OT: No, my pension and Old Age Security will be everything she has. Plus, of course, the Canada Pension Plan survivor's pension. But that won't go very far.

PERCON: For the disadvantaged there are guaranteed income supplements she might be able to qualify for, if she passes a means test.

OT: What! You mean that's what's going to happen if I die? There's got to be another way.

PERCON: Of course there is. The plan offers other types of pension benefits if you want them. For instance, you can make sure that your pension is guaranteed for 15 years, until your wife's 77. Mind you, your pension checks wouldn't be quite as high in the meantime. But at least she'd be covered for a longer period of time.

OT: What happens at 77? She'd still need money.

PERCON: Well, we find that most employees prefer to choose what is known as a "joint and last survivorship" annuity to take care of that.

OT: What's that?

PERCON: It simply means that you will receive a certain pension for the rest of your life and at your death it would be reduced by about one-third and would go to Martha for the rest of her life, no matter how long she lives.

OT: That's more like it. Why didn't you tell me? You had me really worried there.

PERCON: That's exactly why we're having this pension consultation, to help make you aware of all the different kinds of benefits. I think you would be very wise to provide a joint and last survivorship annuity from your pension plan. You must realize, however, that it will cut down your current pension checks a bit.

OT: What does a bit mean?

PERCON: I'll just make a quick calculation here. Let's see, if Martha is 62 now and you want the pension to cover her for the rest of her life, keeping in mind that as a female she's likely to live longer, then we could probably give you a pension of about

$2,000 a month. That's $24,000 a year.

OT: What? Just $24,000? Let's see here. Why, that's only about 48% of my final earnings, not 70%!

PERCON: That's true. But you should consider yourself fortunate because most people who choose this benefit option average about 42% of final earnings. So you're really better off than the average.

OT: But how am I going to tell Martha that we're not going to have $35,000, and more, when I retire? That $24,000 is less than half what I'm making now.

PERCON: Right. But look at the bright side. Your deductions for income tax and other welfare benefits won't be as high as they were.

OT: As high! I thought I wouldn't have to make contributions any more.

PERCON: Well, I'm assuming of course, that you'll want to continue your major medical benefits, and you'll probably want to convert some of your group life insurance benefits. Then there are pension association dues.

OT: Wow. How am I going to get by?

PERCON: The company provides just basic benefits. We assume that all employees have read the terms of the plan. You always have been expected to supplement them with some personal savings.

OT: Do me a favor, will you? Since you're a personnel consultant, could you tell me where I could find a good part-time job somewhere?

Government Pension Payouts: Small and Shaky

Obviously this is a worst-case scenario, especially since so many women today are working and hence have some income of their own, however little. Even so, typical retirees can expect only about 8.5% of their pre-retirement income in Old Age Security payments, and about 15.5% in CPP income. That's not much, and certainly not enough to live on. And the specter of an underfunded CPP continually hovers in the background. Many economists have predicted that the federal government some day won't be able to afford to pay the same kind of CPP benefits as today. This is a hot potato that the government has yet to deal with definitively.

The proportion of people retiring and qualifying for CPP benefits is increasing, and at the same time the proportion of people in the workforce contributing to the plan is declining. And our population's life expectancy continues to increase. This means fewer workers will have to pay more into the plan. Legislated increases are already in the works, but increases of the scope needed to bring the CPP fund up to par probably would not be politically supportable. And no government is likely to risk defeat by pushing through an increase of the size that is really needed. In the meantime, whenever there is a surplus in the CPP fund, the federal government generously lends it to the province at lower-than-market rates or uses it itself to finance its deficit.

I cannot emphasize too much the point that you dare not depend on others, including the government, for your financial well-being. Who knows whether the government will always be able to pay even the modest pension amounts it now does? I can't overemphasize the point: don't assume the government will support you in your retirement years.

A Contradiction in Terms

The expression "job security" is an oxymoron. It's in the same category as "postal service" and "gourmet airline meals" or "government assistance." All are contemporary myths.

Long-term job security is a particularly dangerous myth. If you really believe your job is secure, and you lose it, you could be completely destroyed psychologically. Protect yourself financially by looking at your job as merely a way of earning money; financial security can result only from what you do with that money. You become financially secure by becoming financially independent. You become financially independent by successfully saving and investing part of what you earn from your job, regardless of the eventual outcome of the job.

Why should the terms "job" and "security" be considered so contradictory today? The reasons are legion. Generally speaking, however, political and technological changes spurred by economic and market forces supersede the individual's need for job security. Sometimes the forces move slowly, in some cases almost invisibly, until the last, wrenching moment. But in the long term the individual is always sacrificed on the altar of national (and global) economic need.

Take our so-called free-trade agreement with the United States as an example. Even the federal government now admits there will be considerable loss of jobs as a result of the deal. A major government-appointed commission has confirmed this. Furthermore, the commission recommended that workers displaced as a result of the free-trade pact should receive no more special treatment than anybody else losing a job under other circumstances. Job retraining is the panacea held forth by the commissioners who themselves will never have to undergo retraining.

Unions Don't Always Help

The trend in union activity today is another example of how the individual employee becomes the victim of change. The primary thrust of many unions now is not negotiating more pay and better benefits for members but rather the more basic task of simply preserving jobs. This pressure to maintain the status quo can be carried to ridiculous lengths. Some unions have perversely gone on strike and closed down companies permanently in an attempt to force job security for their members. A glaring example of this was provided by typographical unions in the newspaper business. The unions insisted that their members continue to set type by hand or with antiquated, slow mechanical equipment long after it became apparent that computers operated by lower-paid, non–typographical union employees could do a much more cost-effective job.

The result was featherbedding. Union employees continued doing jobs that were completely unnecessary or redundant. It became so silly that some newspapers paid for the cost of old-fashioned typesetting while they also had the job done by computers. At the end of the day the work done by the typesetters was tossed out. This counter-productive system, generated in the name of job security for typesetters, led to the collapse of some newspapers and the amalgamation of others. Many jobs, more than those just of typesetters, were lost as a result.

This isn't union-bashing. I cite it simply as an example of how desperately many of us can react when we see our job security melting in the face of the latest and hottest changes in technology. In the case of the typesetters, their determination was so strong that, in some cases, they destroyed the very source of the livelihood they were trying to maintain. And typesetters are not the only groups who have tried to defend their jobs to the death with the same futile results.

You'd Better Plan for Change — It's the Course of History

For the first couple of hundred years of our history, apart from the fur trade, the majority of Canadians were employed in some form of agriculture. After two centuries we started to move fairly quickly into the industrial age. The rural population shrank and the urban population grew. The majority of jobs shifted to industry. Coincidentally agriculture became mechanized, and today only about 2% of the population is producing a surplus of food for the country.

Following the turn of this century, industry employed the majority of our population. But because of burgeoning industrial mechanization the number of industrial workers decreased dramatically. In just the past 2 decades we have shifted to a service-oriented society, with service businesses engaging most of the labor force. But even this is changing rapidly too. Thanks to modern electronic advances, one person with a computer can handle the work that it would have taken a dozen to cope with a decade ago. So, it appears that even our ripening information or service society won't need as many employees as it did even 5 to 10 years ago in its earlier stages.

What does all this have to do with financial planning? As any self-employed or part-time worker knows, the only way to become secure in the workplace is to be capable of adjusting to change and continually to improve your skills and performance. That means retraining and re-education, which, only to a minimum extent, is provided without cost to you by governments or corporations. So, you'll have to improve your skills on your own. If you want to go back to school, you'll need money. That means planning ahead so you'll have funds when you need them. If you want to drop out of the business world and start up your own project, you'll need a fair amount of capital. That means even better planning. If you just change jobs, it could mean reduced income for a while — you'll need capital to bridge the gap. What if you want to relocate to another city, or even to another country? That could put severe pressure on your financial resources, pressure you must plan to deal with in advance.

Two-income families today face special problems. One of the two wage-earners may have to relocate either to keep a job or to get a better one. The other partner might have to temporarily give up working to go along. That means a single salary, for at least a while.

Even in a stable industry it is impossible to avoid changes, or to expect a long-term career. Look at banking, the epitome of stability. It's hard to imagine we won't always have banks with us, and if you are a long-term bank employee you might expect a healthy degree of job security. But banking doesn't escape change, even massive change. Computerization and developments like the automatic-teller machines are recent examples. Managers are moved, then removed or replaced by loan officers, divisions restructured, centralized, then decentralized, and unprofitable branches closed. In short, no job is sacred anymore.

It's all done in the name of corporate survival, and if a corporation has to cut costs to survive, it will, regardless of the cost to individual employees. Companies do try to minimize employee dislocation, but, when push comes to shove, corporate survival takes precedence over individual survival every time, on all levels from clerk to management.

Some years ago when I was a vice-president of a large insurance company, I vividly recall an uncomfortable situation in London, England. The City of London had grown so big that it couldn't provide adequate services to companies in its area, so it encouraged firms to relocate elsewhere. Government provided some assistance and grants to encourage firms to move from London's business district to as far as 40 or 50 miles away. My company followed the lead and offered our managers and supervisors financial assistance to relocate. But for many it wasn't practical because two-income families were involved. Some managers had to resign and then try to find other jobs in the City. It was too expensive for companies or government to assist the clerical employees to relocate, so most of them lost their jobs. And insurance companies rank second only to banks in the private-sector stability stakes race.

The spate of corporate mergers and leveraged buyouts also usually results in substantial layoffs, because costs must be cut to reduce the corporate debt. This human toll is seldom mentioned in the pages of our business press. Even so, it is real, and any sensible individual must plan for the possibility of becoming redundant — simply to satisfy the impersonal profit-and-loss statement and balance sheet.

Don't Look Behind — Your Subordinate Is Cheaper

There are lots of other reasons why you could get hurt through a misplaced faith in job security, but they all boil down to that famous (or infamous) bottom line. Take the classic example of a typical 50-year-old male employee who began his career with the firm at age 25 and has risen to middle management or slightly beyond. Normally, if you have that kind of seniority and good standing you'd expect to finish your business life with the same firm.

But quite apart from having to deal with shifting job functions and keeping up with the lightning-fast changes in new technical capabilities required, you are vulnerable if for no other reason than your age. Why? Because you are probably earning in the neighborhood of $50,000 a year. Your understudy, however (there are always one or two of these around), is probably at least 15 years younger and earns perhaps $25,000 to $30,000 a year. It makes economic sense to a lot of companies to get rid of you and replace you with a younger, technically capable subordinate at almost half your salary. Even if you get a generous severance package, the company saves substantially on its payroll costs over time.

Why Benefits Are Not Always Beneficial

If the advantages of reducing a company's payroll by getting rid of middle-aged employees is viable, the advantage of doing the same thing to reduce pension-plan liability is most alluring to cost-conscious corporations. If your company operates a defined-benefit pension plan (the most common in large firms) then you might anticipate receiving maximum pension at age 65. A typical defined-benefits formula might call for a retirement income based on 2% of your salary for each year of service, to a maximum of 70% of final earnings. Here's how an employer might look at that pension benefit if the company is looking for a place to cut costs.

Let's say you are 50 and earn $50,000 a year. You have been with the company for 25 years. If you retired early right now, you would be entitled (at age 65) to 25 × 2%, or 50% of your current earnings from the vested plan. That would amount to $25,000 a year, starting 15 years from now.

If, however, you stayed with the company for another 10 or 15 years, your pension at 65 would be the maximum: 70% of your then current earnings. By that time you probably would be earning around $100,000 a year (remember, an increase of only 7% per year for inflation and merit purposes would double your salary in 10 years). Your pension income then would be about $70,000 a year. So, you can see that the company might be quite happy to give you complete pension benefits vesting now, pat you on the back and let you go off to try and find a comparable job somewhere else.

But that's only part of the story. Chances are that you have been contributing a mandatory 5% of your wages every year to the pension in anticipation of an eventual pension of about $70,000 a year. If you have done so for 25 years, the total amount you have contributed yourself likely will finance your entire pension. If you are let go at age 50, the employer would have to pay little if anything toward your $25,000-a-year pension benefit (based on today's salary) at age 65.

If, however, you carry on with the company to age 65, your pension entitlement will rise to 70% of final earnings. And those final earnings, as mentioned above, will likely be close to $100,000 a year. That means the company must provide 70% of $100,000 a year: $70,000 a year 15 years from now. Your 5% contribution during the next 15 years will not fund the difference between $25,000 and $70,000 a year. It means the employer will have to contribute a substantial amount to fund the difference. As a matter of fact an employer has to place into the plan a phenomenal dollar amount to fund pension-payout growth during the critical years between age 60 and 65. That's why so few employees, especially well-paid ones, last with their companies to age 65.

As we have seen earlier, your actual pension payments would likely be based on an average of perhaps your last 5 years' salary, not your final year's wage. Although this reduces the company's liability somewhat from the 70% figure, the fact remains that additional funding required for employees between the years of 60 and 65 is substantial, and the company will avoid paying it if possible.

At my previous company it was said that more than 20 years had passed since a vice-president had lasted through the full term to age 65. There was always some excuse to retire V-Ps early: corporate reorganization or new management or whatever.

The Golden Handshake Glisters — For the Company

It's not that you'll be terribly ill-treated if you are pushed into early retirement by your company. If you are 50 years old and earning $50,000, you'd probably get a golden handshake worth, perhaps, at least $100,000. The company might even sweeten your severance benefit up to $150,000 in some cases. That would be the equivalent of 3 years' income. The typical formula calls for 1 month's salary for every year of service. So, if you've been on the job for 25 years you might expect about 25 months' salary, or slightly more than $100,000. That might seem a substantial amount to you at your age and you might even think you are being generously treated. But even $100,000 or more costs your employer relatively little compared to what the company would have to pay into the pension plan during the next 15 years if you were to finish your career there.

Benefits: A 2-Way Sword in Terms of Job Security

The high cost of pensions to the company during an employee's later career years is only part of the sad story of diminishing job security, though it is a major part of the story. The other employee benefits also become more expensive the older the employee becomes. The cost to the company of group life and disability income insurances zooms up exponentially as its average payroll age increases. A corporation can keep its disability insurance costs down by getting rid of employees over age 50. The older employee tends to get sicker more seriously and more often. That puts a real strain on the company's benefit-package costs. The idea in managing group insurance from the company's point of view is to level out the contributions so that young people pay more and older people pay less. This means individual employees don't pay their proportionate share of the costs of group life or group health or group disability. So, even in a stable industry with a growth pattern there is every economic reason to get rid of older employees.

The other brutal truth is that most companies want to provide job and promotion opportunities for younger employees. If they don't, they know they will lose them. To keep them they have to make room at the top. So much for job security.

It's Not How Good You Are — It's the Bottom Line

Older employees are seldom less productive than younger ones. To the contrary. Studies from two universities in the United Kingdom indicate that older employees who were let go by their companies were technically more competent and more productive than their younger replacements. So, the lack of job security, ironically, boils down to the bottom line, not productivity or competence.

I have seen this unwritten law operate at first hand in the corporate jungle. I left a senior vice-presidential job at a major financial-services company voluntarily, because I wanted to start the Money Concepts organization. Only 4½ years later, nearly all of the senior executives I had known and worked with at that company were gone. Some were retired early. Some were dismissed outright. Some were offered unacceptable alternative responsibilities. If you have a responsible job and are asked to take on the vice-presidency of paper-clip procurement, you soon get the message and leave, or seek some kind of termination allowance.

As I said before, most employers are not completely cruel, unthinking and unkind. They are simply looking for economies because survival is the first rule of any business. In any event they can't be too unfair because the laws of the land have become more generous toward employees in this situation, so serious injustice is seldom done. Some severance allowances are handsome. But no matter how much you get, it likely will be considerably less than you would have enjoyed if you'd been able to stay on the job with its full salary and benefit package. The government can legislate fair treatment if you lose your job; in a free society it can't legislate job security.

The Do-Your-Own-Thing Urge Requires Planning

While there are many reasons you could lose your job security involuntarily, there are also opportunities for which you might choose to give up such security. There is an increasing trend today for people at almost any age to break away from the business world to do their own thing. That could mean relocating to another city or country, switching to a different career, taking a sabbatical to improve their education, or to write books; or just to travel to places they have never been but want to see before they become too old to do so.

Such people are unlikely to derive a great deal of satisfaction working for a large corporation. The thought of working for one or two large firms for their entire working career is unthinkable to them. So they don't develop a lot of loyalty to their current employer because they don't intend to stay there very long. They simply rent out their services to that company in return for a reasonable wage, always knowing that they'll move on to pursuing their own career goals some day.

If you are such an employee, you have special need for intricate financial planning because you will have to fund your own endeavors when you launch them.

Another Myth: Income Requirements Drop After Retiring

A prevailing myth or misconception about personal money management is the assumption that you won't need as much money when you retire as you do when you're working because you won't have to face the added costs of going to work (transportation, wardrobe, lunches). In fact nothing could be farther from the truth. More often most of us live up to our income during our careers and it's very difficult for us to have to adjust to a sudden drop of, say, 52% in income just because we have reached that magical date at age 65.

It's quite easy to build a case that when you retire you'll actually need a pension income not only greater than 52% of your pre-retirement income, but as much as 110% or even 125%. Whether you're employed or self-employed, don't you sometimes dream, or daydream, that when you reach 65 you'll suddenly, finally, gain the freedom and the sheer luxury of having time (and money) to do all those things you never got around to when you were working? But, unless you augment the typical company pension income from your own resources, you'll have less money than at any other time in your life.

Another popular money-management myth is that you will be completely free of debt by the time you are 65, so you really won't need as much income. That assumes, of course, that nobody after age 45 will take on a 25-year mortgage, or have any children to educate or won't still be supporting children living at home. I do not believe these assumptions hold water for many people; often at 65 you are still paying down a mortgage, or paying off debts built up while sending children to increasingly expensive post-secondary educational institutions. And what about parents who have disadvantaged or disabled children at home? Or aging parents who have to be provided for?

Yet Another Retirement Myth

Have you ever thought that when you retire you will sell your home and use the capital to live on, or at least invest it to generate income? Don't forget you have to live somewhere and renting can be very, very costly. If you own a house in a high-value area like Toronto or Vancouver, you might get a good price when you sell. If you are prepared to move to a small town many miles away, where housing costs perhaps are one-third those of a large urban area, you might be able to pocket a sizable difference.

But it doesn't always happen that way. The older you are the more difficult you probably will find it to adjust to new surroundings and new friends. I hear a lot of sad tales of people who sell their houses in the city and buy mobile homes in Florida's interior, thinking it won't cost them as much to live there. It might not, though it always costs more than you think it will. But only too often they discover they dislike the neighbors, the bugs or the climate, or they find it difficult to make friends. They are thousands of miles from their families and grandchildren as well as many of the interests that they have developed during their lives, such as theater, sports, craft clubs or the like. If you haven't planned to supplement your company and government pensions with your own savings, you could be stuck in Florida or somewhere else with low house prices but a place, you belatedly realize, that you cannot abide. If you don't own a house or a condominium, you already know how much a regular rent check drains your resources.

It's best to be realistic and accept the fact that the purpose of company and government pensions is not to supply all of life's comforts to all retirees. They are designed to be no more than a safety net — to provide a basic minimum retirement income so you won't starve. They never promised you a rose garden, or round-the-world trips. If you have a government and/or a company pension, you simply have a base — a base to which you must add your own assets to construct a comfortable income structure — and your own financial freedom.

11

Inflation: The Enemy That Never Sleeps

There's a story told about the middle-aged man who contracted an incurable disease. But he believed in the eventual triumph of medical science and of cryonics (the practice of freezing organisms for storage in the expectation of future revival and use). So, he arranged to have his body frozen. Sure enough, 30 years later, scientists discovered a cure for his particular disease. At the appropriate time he was unfrozen and brought back to life. His illness was then cured and he looked forward to getting on with the rest of his life.

That, however, is not the happy ending to this story. The first thing the man did after he was thawed, revived and cured was to phone his old broker long distance in New York. His broker excitedly informed the man that things had gone very well during the past 30 years and that his portfolio had grown from a rather modest amount to a couple of million dollars. The man, of course, was ecstatic. He could hardly believe his good fortune. As he was wondering what to do with his new-found wealth, the operator came on the line and said, "Your time is up. Please deposit $25,000 for 3 minutes."

This story exemplifies the unrelenting reality of inflation as well as any. We all want the so-called benefits that inflation is thought by some to bring; but we don't want to put up with the problems.

To many of us, inflation is only a word economists and business writers love to use. We think that if it does touch us personally it might mean that food costs go up a little but to offset that we'll get a lot more interest from our savings accounts and higher wages from our employers to compensate.

However, in an insidious way inflation creates more problems than it solves. You tend to ignore it, especially when you set goals for financial or retirement plans. But you cannot ignore it because it inexorably eats away much of what you have or hope to have, especially when you are on a fixed income after retiring.

Inflation is deceptive, too, in the false expectations it stimulates. Everyone knows about the soaring value of real estate in recent years. I recall my father purchasing a home in Brandon, Manitoba, for $600 cash in 1939. It was a good-sized house with 4 bedrooms, in those days enough room to raise a family of 6. He sold it in 1944 for $3,600 and bought a home in Winnipeg for $5,600. This was a huge structure — 3 floors, 6 bedrooms — in a fashionable neighborhood. It sold for $12,000 in 1951. I suppose that house today would cost me more than $250,000.

And that's nothing compared to what's happened in Toronto and Vancouver. You might eagerly anticipate the huge sum you'll get for your home if you sold it next week. But the high cost of replacing it would dampen your enthusiasm like a cold shower. It's not so bad if you were to sell and not rebuy (perhaps rent), but housing prices have gone completely out of sight, making home ownership impossible for many would-be first-time purchasers.

A 1989 survey of home ownership revealed that in the United States, and I think this would hold true for Canada, too, more homes were owned by couples *without* children than were owned by couples *with* children. It takes a 2-income family unsaddled with childrearing costs to make home-ownership a reality for most young people today.

What's Wrong With Zero Inflation?

This means our standard of living is continually eroding. And it continues to erode when the rate of inflation is anything beyond 0%. I don't know how our central bank and governments can make happy noises, as they sometimes do, about wrestling inflation to the ground from the terrible 14% levels of the early 1980s to near 4%. Why not 4.5%? Or 3.7%? That's a little like admitting that you feel so much better now because you used to hit yourself on the head with a hammer 14 times a day, and now you only do it 4 times a day, which makes life slightly more bearable. Everybody's target, in fact, especially governments', should be 0% inflation if they really are serious about dealing with the problem and protecting their constituents. But they all want to be re-elected, and to get re-elected they have to spend money — your money. They always spend more than they have, so they print more, stimulating inflation. It's a never-ending spiral upwards, so you had better get used to it, and factor it into your plans.

This becomes especially important in view of the government's impending Goods and Services Tax. The GST undoubtedly will send the inflation rate reeling upwards. How far and how long is the subject of constant discussion among editorial writers and economists. Specific figures or even close estimates are impossible at the time of writing, or even at the best of times when it comes to different economists making forecasts. Since the legislation is still in proposal stage and likely will have changed considerably before it becomes law, there is one thing you can be sure of: higher costs and higher inflation.

A University of Western Ontario economics professor, David Laidler, testifying in 1989 before the House of Commons standing committee on finance and economic affairs, asked, "Is a 4% or 5% inflation rate worth all the trouble to get rid of?"

You bet it is. Professor Laidler went on to cite a couple of examples to illustrate "why it is not totally silly to be concerned with 4% inflation:

"Consider someone retiring on an unindexed pension at the age of 65. A 4% inflation rate in round numbers is enough to reduce the purchasing power of the pension by about 25% by the time that person gets to the age of 70. That's a fairly big cut.

"Secondly, people tend to forget that inflation interacts with the tax structure, which does some funny things to interest rates. For example, suppose that I as a saver want a 2% after-tax real return on my savings, and suppose that I am in a 50% tax bracket. If there is no inflation, that means I need a before-tax nominal rate of interest of 4%. But if there is a 4% inflation rate, I need a 6% after-tax return on my assets to get that 2% real rate. And that means I must have a *12% before-tax rate of return* [italics mine] on my nominal assets.

"In other words, there are pressures coming from the interaction of the tax system with inflation that mean that nominal interest rates tend to get pushed up by more than a simple inflation premium. That is worth bearing in mind."

Professor Laidler is oh so right. He appropriately brings up that 2-headed monster, inflation and taxation. I'll talk about taxation as it affects your personal financial planning in the next chapter, but what you have to understand is that inflation does not just add to your burden of taxation, it multiplies it exponentially. It's a bit like a first-year chemistry procedure when you add what appears to be one innocent-looking element to another and suddenly produce an explosion that ricochets the test-tube cork off the classroom ceiling. Or like drinking alcohol and taking antihistamines at the same time. The effect of each on the other is many times more powerful than the simple sum of two elements added together.

In my seminars I often ask the audience what issue of Canada Savings Bonds they would prefer if they had their choice of all the series of CSBs over many years. Invariably the hands shoot up and the answer is, "Well, Series 36, brought out in 1981." Then I ask them, "Why do you make that choice?"

"The rate of interest on those bonds was 19.5%."

Hard to argue with that logic, right? A rate of 19.5% sounds mighty attractive. But then I always ask, "Assuming that that interest rate was fully exposed to taxation and you were in a 50% tax bracket, how much of that 19.5% was yours to keep after the government gets its hands on its part first?"

Well, they generally say, the mathematics are pretty simple: you divide 19.5 by 50%, giving half to the government and keeping half yourself. You've got 9¾% left. Still not bad.

"But," I continue, "does anybody know what the rate of inflation was in 1981?"

The answer is about 12½%. So what was the net rate of return after inflation? The bottom line: minus 2¾%." CSBs a good investment in 1981? Not on your life.

All of which means, of course, that you cannot consider interest rates alone when assessing what makes a good investment. Supposing that you could earn 10% interest on your money today, and you have no tax shelter, and the rate of inflation is 5%. Doesn't that sound better than the good old days when you could only get 5% on your money and the rate of inflation was, say, 1%? The quick answer is to go for the 10%. But apply the maths again. You get 10% and you pay 50% of it in tax so you have 5% left as a nominal rate of return. But with inflation at 5% you have just broken even.

On the other hand, if you earn only 5% on your investment, and you pay half of that to the government, you would be left with only 2.5% as your rate of return. But with inflation only at 1%, you would end up with 1.5%. That's better than today's returns, and better than

1981 when you got 19.5% in interest but ended up in the hole.

Inflation's False Promise

Most people don't see it that way, though, because somehow the general conception is that inflation will stimulate a rise in income that will bail you out of your financial difficulties. Let me tell you what I mean. A couple of years ago in Prince Edward Island, my company was opening a new financial-planning center. I was on hand to help and subsequently was invited onto a local radio phone-in talk show on money matters.

One young couple phoned and described at some length the problems they had trying to match their income to expenses. After discussing the topic for a little while, Robert, the husband, dismissed the whole problem: "Well, I think we are going to be okay anyway." The reason, he explained, was that he was expecting a year-end raise at work. I asked him how much he expected to get.

"Probably about 6%," he said.

"Robert," I asked, "how much are you making now?" It turned out to be about $30,000 a year. He was pinning his hopes on that $30,000 bumped up by 6% — an extra $1,800 coming in throughout the following year. That would mean something like $150 a month, or $75 every two weeks. He and his wife felt this was kind of comforting, especially considering their budget was then consistently falling short of balancing each month by $50 or $75.

Cathy said, "I guess it's kind of nice working for a big firm where you have these fairly regular economic increases."

I decided to ask a few more questions. "Robert and Cathy," I asked, "why do you think employers give these regular raises?" They thought for a while and they replied that they guessed it was mostly to cover the extra costs of living due to inflation. At that time inflation was running at about 5%.

"Well, why don't you take a pencil and a piece of paper and go through a little mathematical exercise with me for a moment," I said to them. "Let's suppose, Robert, that you do get that extra $150 per month. How much will your company deduct from the $150 and send directly to Revenue Canada, before you see a penny?"

He paused for a moment, then said, "Oh, about 33 to 40%."

"Okay," I went on, "let's write down that Revenue Canada gets

$50 of your increase. That leaves you with $100. Correct? Now, how much extra would be deducted from your paycheck," I continued, "for group insurance, pension plan contributions and the rest?"

He figured perhaps another $15.

"Okay," I said, "now your raise is down to $85 a month, right?"

Affirmative again, but with a little hesitation this time.

I asked them how they expected their costs to increase next year if the rate of inflation stayed at 5%.

"Well," Robert said, "$30,000 a year is about $2,500 per month, or $1,250 every 2 weeks. If you add 5% inflation to that, it comes to about $62 every 2 weeks."

I instructed him to subtract that additional $62 from the $85 remaining from the raise. That left them $23 ahead from a $150 raise. "Now," I asked, "were you by any chance thinking of making any major purchases because of the extra cash you'll have after Robert's raise?"

They admitted, a little sheepishly now, that they had been thinking of moving Cathy into a newer car. The additional finance charges they figured would probably only come to $100 per month.

I summed up for them: "Robert and Cathy, you're falling short of balancing your budget now by $75 a month. You're thinking of paying $100 more every month in car payments than you are paying right now. Robert's raise is going to net you $23. How do you expect to do all of these things without falling even farther behind?"

I got in a plug for my profession. "It sounds like you need a good financial planner," I ended.

Inflation Is Insidious, Invidious and Pervasive

Robert and Cathy are not at all unusual in the way they think about money and inflation. We all like to anticipate more income and higher assets because we expect to get a raise. Or because our house appreciates in value by 7 or 8% every year. That tends to make us feel rather good. But we almost always fail to look at the other side of the coin — the startling amount that inflation and tax push up expenses.

For instance, there is nothing more rewarding at times than to sit down and look at your pension or RRSP contributions and note how they have increased in value. Isn't it great that the accumulated amount is growing by 10% to 12% a year? But what about the other side of the coin? How much are we going to need at retirement time in inflated dollars? Look at Figure 12; it will help put your pension requirements into perspective. The chart shows current income requirements and compares them to the dollar amounts you need after inflation to provide the same amount of income 5, 10, 20 and 30 years hence. For example, if you need $20,000 a year to maintain a reasonable standard of living today, and if inflation averages 6%, you'd need about $70,000 to live the same way 20 years from now.

IMPACT OF INFLATION

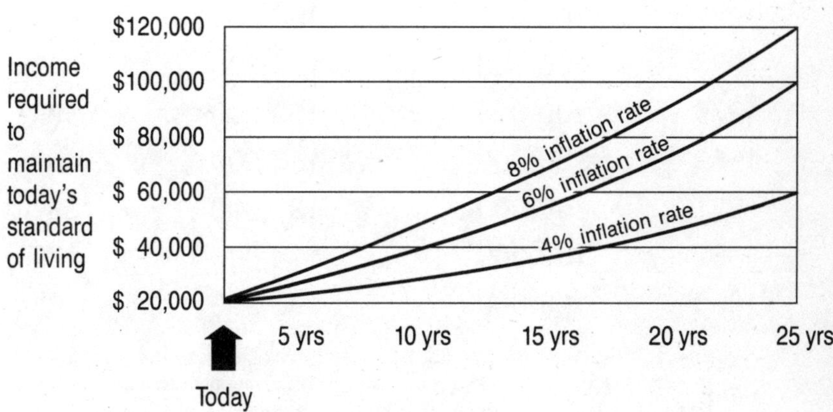

Figure 5: Inflation not only eats into retirement savings and pensions, it can devastate them. The chart shows how much MORE money you will need to maintain today's standard of living, given different inflation rates.
(Source: Printed with permission of Vernon-Longman Publishing, inc.)

I've got nothing good to say about inflation. It permeates not just our take-home pay but just about everything we have and everything we do. Its effect on low-income compared to higher-income taxpayers is especially invidious. Even your life insurance doesn't escape the ravages of inflation either and insurance is an essential component of everybody's financial plan, as you will understand a couple of chapters from now. If you haven't reviewed your life insurance for 2 or 3 years, and many people don't, you are probably underinsured. Inflation alone guarantees that. Figure 13 shows what happens if you don't review, and add to, your life insurance from time to time.

INFLATION CAN BE FATAL

Year of last insurance review	Assumed amount of life insurance owned	Amount of life insurance required in 1984 to provide the same benefits	Percentage increase required
1973	$100,000	$267,000	167%
1974	100,000	248,000	148%
1975	100,000	218,000	118%
1976	100,000	202,000	102%
1977	100,000	188,000	88%
1978	100,000	174,000	74%
1979	100,000	159,000	59%
1980	100,000	146,000	46%
1981	100,000	133,000	33%
1982	100,000	118,000	18%
1983	100,000	106,000	6%

Figure 6: Inflation can have a fatal effect on your insurance protection too. This table assumes an average annual inflation rate of 6% (which is our actual 20-year average).
(Source: Printed with permission of Vernon-Longman Publishing, inc.)

Is It Really That Bad?

Admit it now. Haven't you assured yourself more than once that your personal cost of living doesn't increase at the same rate as the CPI cost-of-living index? The official cost of living is an index based on the cost of a standard basket of goods said to be used by most people. But you know you can cut back here and there on some of the items in the basket. You don't buy a new car every 12 months or renew your mortgage every year, so you don't have those additional costs (car and mortgage costs are in the official basket, too). You tend to take notice of the official cost-of-living figure when it suits you, perhaps during a political discussion at a Saturday-night party, and ignore it otherwise.

In theory, I would have to agree with you. But in practice I don't. Why? Simply because our expectations tend to rise with the level of our income. You are not so different from Robert and Cathy who anticipated Robert's raise by immediately starting to think about how they would improve their lifestyle by buying Cathy a newer car.

Cars, incidentally, are excellent examples of our very human tendency to slide our expectations up notch by notch, almost without thinking about it. Take a standard model car and its cost a year ago, 5 years ago, 10 years ago, 15 years ago. For example, in 1960 I bought a shiny new Ford Fairlane car from a dealer in downtown Toronto. It was beautiful. It was brand-new. And it cost me $2,100. A similar car today would cost $15,000 to $18,000. But today my expectations are different and, partly because of my increased income, I am no longer content to drive a Ford Fairlane or its equivalent. I can be as easily seduced (sometimes more easily) by features and design changes that I never dreamed about years ago. Yesterday's luxury becomes today's necessity. Marketers and manufacturers depend on it. Many people wouldn't think of buying a car today without air conditioning, power windows and a FM radio, not to speak of a stereo cassette deck and perhaps a CD player. Sometimes you don't even have a choice. Many of yesterday's luxuries are not luxuries at all but are built into today's cars as standard features. But they are also built into the price. Thus our transportation costs escalate.

Our rising level of expectation applies to our children's education too. A college education is considered essential now. At one time it was a luxury that only a few people could afford. But we accept the principle of "universal access" for all who can qualify for admission to university and we expect the government to provide that access. Whether we pay for it ourselves directly or the government does so by adding to our tax burden, the higher expectation persists. And that adds to our cost of living.

Would you buy a new house today without making sure that it had a washer, dryer, dishwasher, refrigerator or a stove and oven as part of the deal? These are now standard features in new homes. Yet, in previous generations our grandparents and even parents worked for years before they could afford the equivalent of a large-capacity, frost-free freezer chest and a microwave oven.

So it goes, on and on and on and on. And up and up and up. We expect more and we demand more. If we don't get what we want, we goon strike, or we badger our employer for more income to fuel inflation. Everybody plays the game of catch-up. But with the tax base being what it is, seldom do we ever catch up.

What happens when inflation runs rampant and governments can no longer control it? Then you have economic chaos. Governments will print more money to meet the needs of government and this devalues the dollar.

Let me give you an example. In March 1988, my family and I flew to Acapulco for spring break. The sun was a scorcher, and the town and beaches were jam packed. Apparently we hit the town during what is known there as *Semana Santa*, Holy Week. The beaches were awash with not only tourists but also Mexicans from Mexico City who were visiting their holiday condominiums to get away from the horrendous heat of the capital city.

One day on the beach we met a Mexican businessman and his wife. Our conversation soon drifted to money, interest rates and taxation. I had noticed in the papers that interest rates were very high in Mexico, and he agreed: "Oh yes. There is no problem whatsoever in getting 35% to 40% interest on your money even if you invest it for only 30 or 40 days."

I was amazed at the rate. But when he told me that the interest earned was tax-free, I was astounded. He explained, "If you didn't provide interest tax free then no one would invest any money."

It would all be invested in the black market or in some way to escape government scrutiny, he said. Banks or government securities, bonds and the like were the last things people would use or buy. If you got 40% on your money and had to pay half to the government in tax, you'd end up with only 20%. With inflation running at 25% to 40% it doesn't take much brainpower to see you'd be in the hole before you started. The only way investors could come out ahead would be to get 70% or 80% on their money so they would have enough left to at least match the rate of inflation. But, he added, if interest rates were to go that high they would fuel even higher inflation, perhaps approaching 100%. So the government preferred the approach of not taxing interest income to keep the country's apparent inflation rate within reason.

Even in the most tightly controlled society there is still some inflation. In the global community a country cannot isolate itself from inflation in other countries. So, inflation is insidious. You must protect yourself against it. How do you do that, apart from expecting and demanding less from yourself and from your governments? Two things I can suggest:

1. Make investments whose value increases along with or faster than the rate of inflation and which might not be taxable at the maximum rates. Housing is a pretty good investment in that category. But equities are perhaps the best. A well-managed portfolio of common stocks over a long period of time is about the best hedge against inflation that you could have. And the worst are short-term instruments (GICs, bank accounts, even treasury or investor's accounts). The income from these is fully taxable.
2. Recognize inflation for what it is and plan accordingly.

How do you choose among these possibilities, and all the hype and propaganda in the media extolling individual investments? That's why financial planners are in business — their business is helping you focus on your real needs and advising which investments might best fulfill those needs.

12

Government: Your Unwanted Planning Partner

"*The art of taxation consists in so plucking the goose as to obtain the largest amount of feathers with the least amount of hissing.*" So said Jean Colbert, seventeenth-century French statesman and financial reformer. His remark was right on the mark then, and it is just as appropriate today. In fact, successive Canadian governments have proven themselves front-running pluckers par excellence — in a world full of major-league tax gatherers. And Canadian taxpayers remain remarkable docile and hiss-less as government hands slip deeper and deeper to extract more and more of our golden feathers.

Just how deep? Well the Fraser Institute in Vancouver advises us every year when "Freedom Day" is. Freedom Day is the day when the average Canadian family finish paying in taxes all the income they have earned to date that year. Only after that date can they start keeping the money they are earning for themselves. The Institute includes not only income tax but provincial, municipal and federal sales taxes. Tax Freedom Day varies from province to province, but recently it has been falling around the early part of July — between July 7 and 11. So, for more than half a year, if you are an average Canadian, you work solely to pay taxes and nothing but taxes, to support your governments.

The Fraser Institute also suggests that Tax Freedom Day should actually be mid- to late-August if we want to be realistic and pay the amount of tax we really should be paying to eliminate our various government deficits. As a nation we spend more than we take in, creating huge deficits; then we borrow (or create more paper money) to finance the shortfall. The only way to get rid of these deficits and to balance our budgets is either to raise taxes or cut government spending. Or both. Since governments make the decisions, you know what choice they will make.

Freedom Day has crept inexorably later and later over the years. In the early to mid 1960s it fell some time in May. Because of its rapid growth and infiltration into our lives, the word taxation elicits a strong emotional reaction from most people and it is not a positive one. We have "sin" taxes on alcohol, cars, gasoline, tobacco and sundry luxury items. We have a raft of hidden taxes (26% compared to just 5% in the United States) about which much was revealed when the Canadian government started talking in 1989 about introducing a goods and services tax. The more the tax is hidden, the less accountable legislators are to Parliament and the voters. Contributions to the Canada Pension Plan constitute another form of taxation. Then we have the various provincial hospitalization plan premiums, unemployment insurance premiums and on and on and on — all different forms of taxation. Accordingly, tax avoidance, or at least minimizing tax, has grown into a significant industry.

It has been pointed out more than once by economists that taxation in this country could be significantly simplified by applying a flat rate of tax on all incomes, and eliminating all the other taxes. But no government could afford to be so logical. That would be political suicide. We would then realize just how much and how substantial all our hidden and indirect taxes have been all along!

Although it requires an accountant (and a specialized one at that), to properly master the complicated and ever-shifting world of taxation, you as a taxpayer must become relatively conversant with the Income Tax Act so you can determine what is deductible and what is not. If you don't, you'll be helping the government pluck your own feathers, and nobody will feel sorry for you. As a U.S. court pronounced in 1904, "Taxes are what we pay for a civilized society." But it is quite legitimate to minimize what you have to pay. A widely publicized precedent for this was established centuries ago in British common law. In essence the judgment stated that while citizens must pay taxes, they could arrange their affairs in such a way that they paid the minimum amount, and nobody was obligated to pay more than they absolutely had to.

Unfortunately most of us don't arrange our affairs to pay the minimum amount of tax. I'm not talking here about high-priced tax attorneys and accountants ferreting out every last tax loophole for the well-heeled individual or corporation. I am talking about you as an individual using a little common sense and a basic knowledge of tax rules when it comes to filling in your annual forms.

For instance, you often pay too much tax when your company deducts it from your paycheck throughout the year. You have to make sure your company knows your exact tax status — married, widowed, number of children and ages, how many others you might be supporting, etc. The company can then come closer to the precise amount to deduct for your taxes. For example, if their records say that you are single and you are really married, then too much is deducted.

Also, if you are making contributions to a group RRSP at work, you also might be paying too much tax every payday. Did you know that you have the option of filling out a special form that shows the government you are contributing? This qualifies you for a lower tax deduction, and thus a higher take-home pay. Not many of my clients have taken advantage of this form and so they have paid too much tax every payday through the year. So, the government benefits from using *your* money for an entire year without paying you any interest. You should be the one to invest that money and collect interest — after all, you earned it.

Not keeping every medical receipt is another simple but foolish foible many of my clients have. Consequently they don't bother to claim all the medical deductions allowed on their tax form because they think they won't qualify. I don't mean just dental bills, but receipts for all prescriptions, eyeglasses, orthotics, prosthetics and many other items and services. Deductible expenses include the premiums you pay for a private group medical plan (but not provincial hospitalization plans). It is especially important to keep all these medical receipts because since the 1988 tax reform, medical deductions are more generous for some taxpayers.

And did you know that you can deduct for tax purposes a portion of your children's summer camp costs under the guise of child care?

Because individuals cannot control the level of taxes or the rate of inflation, planners usually advise their clients to invest in land, real estate and in equities of corporations. This type of investment usually results in the least amount of tax, and tends to keep pace with inflation. Some people insist on keeping their money in short-term deposits and in debt instruments such as guaranteed investment certificates, bonds and in bank savings accounts. Those who do will be hit by taxation immediately and such investments seldom offset the ravages of inflation. The idea is to keep only a minimum amount in short-term savings, only enough to cover short-term emergencies and to pay monthly bills.

An RRSP Is Not Necessarily the Ultimate Tax Shelter

The only exception to this approach is continually to turn over short-term instruments inside an RRSP. This can help you offset the worst effects of inflation and taxation by allowing your savings to compound in a tax-sheltered environment for some time. But, keep in mind this is only a temporary saving because eventually the tax man cometh — when you mature your plan or when you die. And then your estate can be hit hard with deferred taxes.

In that connection it always amazes me how many pensioners I talk with who continue to defer tax by rolling over all or some of their pension income into RRSPs or spousal RRSP or RRIFs. Some of them want to leave as much money to their heirs as possible. Some simply hate paying tax. To me this aversion to paying tax is a clear example of a national financial phobia although it is not unique to Canadians. Some people who roll over their RRSPs or RRIFs seem to be comforted by the thought that if they die, their tax-sheltered assets will pass to their spouses in full. In many cases that is true. But they forget that is as far as it goes. The government has immense patience and is prepared to bide its time until the surviving spouse dies. Then the estate is fully taxable. That means any RRSPs and RRIFs have to be matured and the proceeds taken into the deceased person's current year's income. The estate's tax bill can be horrendously high, and surviving beneficiaries might not benefit from deferral. Nor has the deceased enjoyed the extra income when he or she was alive, having squirreled it away back into the tax shelter. The only winner is Revenue Canada.

Consider the hypothetical case of a married man who builds up an RRSP and doesn't draw from it even in retirement. His idea is to pass as much along to his children or nieces and nephews as possible. Upon his death the plan's assets are about $200,000. The RRSP is passed along to his widow and is not taxable. She, having another meager source of income and remembering her late husband's wish to settle as much in the children as possible, keeps the RRSP intact and also does not draw from it. After 5 years the plan's assets have risen to $250,000, and she dies. At this point the RRSP is fully taxable. Since it is considered income in that year, the estate is in the highest tax bracket. The children and other beneficiaries will be lucky if they end up sharing half of what is left.

In a case like this it is better to convert all or part of the RRSP to regular income during the lifetime of the plan-holder, or at least during the widow's lifetime. Then they can enjoy a more comfortable lifestyle. One alternative is to mature part of the RRSP every year and give the children cash gifts. The tax is apt to be less if the plan-holder is in a lower tax bracket.

There Is More to Life Than Tax Reduction

If you rely solely on a tax accountant to advise you, remember that their training tends to teach them that a tax reduction is a person's sole purpose in life. If you look at your income that way, you could be seriously shortchanging yourself. Consider the not-uncommon case of a person in the highest tax bracket rushing out to buy almost any kind of tax shelter late in the year for the *sole purpose* of minimizing tax. It's often not the wise thing to do because the investor is focusing on the amount of immediate tax write-off, and that can cloud judgment. An investment must be judged on its own merits *as an investment*. If it isn't solid, you can lose more than you save with the tax write-off. We do stupid things like this because we have an emotional aversion, albeit a natural one, to give up our hard-earned money to the government.

Limited real estate partnerships are a particularly favored ploy for this purpose and most of them are sold at year-end, in November and December. Even investors in high tax brackets, those you'd expect to have access to expert financial advice, frequently leave it until the last minute. Then they jump in without much thought about the basic value of the investment itself. But the old adage applies to all investments: make an investment only if it is a sound one and not because it might reduce your tax.

One of the stories I enjoy about tax centers on the legislature building in Charlottetown, P.E.I., known as Province House. The sandstone floors are extremely old and worn. In fact, in some places in the building deep grooves have been abraded into the floor. The grooves are deepest and most noticeable leading into the taxation office. The islanders today insist that the grooves are deepest in front of the tax office because taxpayers waiting in line over the years show their reluctance to pay by dragging their feet as they slowly move forward in line.

Our Attitudes Are Wrong

Our reluctance to pay tax sometimes assumes strange forms. One of the strangest, and silliest, is our feeling of celebration when we get a tax-refund check several months after we have submitted our tax forms. The government actually gives us money back! Why can't we realize we are getting our own money back because during the year we cheerfully let the government deduct too much from our paychecks each month? The fact that the government had use of that money for a long period of time without paying interest on it usually doesn't occur to us. All we think of is getting back that fat check from the government in early summer.

Perhaps some people think of it as enforced savings. That may be, but it is the poorest form of enforced saving, if for no other reason than it does not earn any interest for you. And how often, when the check finally does arrive, do we blow it all on celebrating out on the town and perhaps a new wardrobe instead of socking it into an RRSP?

Some taxpayers don't even wait for the government to send them the check; they deal with private-sector tax-preparation organizations that advance them a refund right away, minus a hefty commission, of course. In many cases the fees these companies earn for preparing our taxes are secondary to the amount that they earn from rebating income-tax refunds to impatient taxpayers.

As I've stressed earlier, in Chapter 9, the same cloudy train of thought about avoiding tax applies to the way many of us buy RRSPs. It is safe to say that most RRSP-buyers really don't give too much thought to what they buy, so long as they do make a contribution, usually at the last minute. Look at the lineups at banks and trust companies on the deadline days of February 28 or 29 each year. If you can't afford the whole amount in a lump sum in January, when you really should be adding to our RRSPs, you should make monthly contributions from then on.

The financial industry gears itself up for what it calls RRSP season starting in December. Most people make their deposits in the last two weeks before the end-of-February deadline. To reduce your tax load there are other legitimate methods and techniques, as a good financial planner can show you. You should take advantage of them.

Taxes in one form or another have been with us from the beginning of civilization. Taxation is a monumental fixture in our lives. Benjamin Franklin put it succinctly in the eighteenth century: "In this world nothing is certain but death and taxes." In Canada, income tax was introduced during the First World War as a "temporary" measure to help finance our war effort. But don't expect our provincial and federal governments to phase out this "temporary" measure. Governments may shoot themselves in the foot occasionally, but never in the head. Successful politicians understand human motivation very well. They know instinctively what psychologists study for years to learn: most people will react to things that are personal, immediate and certain. That which is deferred, of general interest and uncertain we don't give high priority to. If a particular measure passed through Parliament is going to hit me in my pocketbook immediately, then I rebel and resist, and I will speak through the ballot box in the next election. If I think that measure is going to hit other people and may not even affect them for some time to come, then I will support that measure and will support the politician who proposes it.

Politicians also understand our heritage. Canadians tend to go along with what central authority (read "government") proposes, more so than do, say, Americans. This stems from our "garrison mentality," as the eminent scholar Northrop Frye points out. After all, Canadians had a colonial master a century longer than the Americans did. So our obedience to central authority had a century longer to become ingrained into our national psyche. Since, as Tennyson said, "I am a part of all that I have met," such elements of our psyche are likely to be with us for some time yet.

It would take a momentous effort to free ourselves from our past, or at least to shrug off the parts of it that lay such a heavy financial burden on us today. Perhaps we should start relying less on central governments and more on ourselves as individuals. If we could do that in the realm of personal financial planning, we could become more prosperous both individually and collectively as a nation.

Entire books have been written about how to minimize your taxes, but I don't have space to deal with the subject to any extent here. The point I want to make in this book is that taxation is a major factor in every individual's life. It is complicated and thinking about it is depressing, but it won't go away, and you must deal with it. You must consider its effects in the personal financial plan you put together.

13

Life Insurance: Cornerstone of a Financial Plan

You wouldn't dream of not insuring your home to its maximum limit. In fact, if you carry a mortgage on a house, for example, the mortgage company will insist the house be covered. You wouldn't dream of not insuring your 4-cylinder Honda economy or your 6-cylinder Buick mid-size car adequately. Or your $5,000 10-hp Mercury outboard aluminum runabout or your $50,000 C and C sloop, if you have one. And the contents of your apartment or house, however modest. By covering those special assets with insurance you ensure their replacement if catastrophe strikes.

But what about protecting the biggest and most special asset of all: your ability to earn income? Your own and/or your family's economic future depends largely on you and your continued income. The hoary old spectacle of a modern-day Simon Legree foreclosing on a widow who can't pay the mortgage is perhaps a little out of date. But I have yet to hear of a financial institution waiving mortgage payments permanently just because the mortgagor died.

If you have no way of replacing a possible loss or severe reduction of income, you are building your and/or your family's financial plan on a shaky foundation. It is missing an essential cornerstone and could tumble down about their ears when you are no longer there to help prop it up with your earning power.

Life insurance, of course, is that cornerstone. And because it is such an important element in the foundation of your personal financial plan, you must know something about it.

Most of you probably consider life insurance a pretty boring subject, right? And confusing, too? Besides, you probably have some insurance through your benefits package at work or directly from an insurance company. So you have the cornerstone well in place.

But have you? Canadians (like Americans and Japanese) are among the best-insured people per capita in the world. But frequently we don't have the right type of life insurance. And more often, we don't recognize the need to review our coverage regularly when our circumstances change. If you are an average Canadian, you probably have grossly underinsured your life and at the same time have been insurance-happy about some aspects of your car and home and placed too much coverage on them. This probably is due less to your modesty and more to ignorance of the facts and of what you really should be doing.

For instance, did you know that the amount of life insurance carried by all Canadians is 1½ times our national income? And that most studies on the subject reveal that the amount of life insurance required by a breadwinner is between 5 and 10 times annual income? This means that if you earn $40,000 a year, you should have between $200,000 to $400,000 of life insurance, according to the experts. Even if you do have that much, read on. There are a few other things you should know.

For instance, you don't have to die (for your family) to benefit from life insurance. I recall my early working days, when I was out beating the British Columbia bushes for business. One evening, at a remote construction camp, I got talking with a grader foreman from a road-building crew. In those days they were still blasting through the mountains to build or improve the highways that today's tourists take for granted. We were talking about financial matters, of course, and after a while he showed me his portfolio of stocks and bonds. It was very impressive indeed. As a matter of fact the dividend and interest income from that portfolio matched the earnings from his job. He and his wife were able to lead a very comfortable life as a result and had no financial worries for the future.

I asked him how he had managed to build up enough savings to get started on such a portfolio. The answer: it all began with the proceeds of a small permanent life insurance policy his father had bought for him when he was born. Unlike many young men he had resisted the temptation to squander the savings, or cash-value, part of the policy when he became 21. Instead he invested it, and invested it wisely. He built his portfolio up and could have retired in comfort in his 50s. He had profited substantially from the legacy of his father's foresight.

But many people don't live to tell such tales, and one of the reasons that so many of us are reluctant to learn much about life insurance is that life insurance is really death insurance and death is not a very pleasant prospect to contemplate. Few people under 50 think much about death, especially premature death. When you are young, you assume that the natural effervescence of life you feel at that age will last forever, if you think about such things at all. When you are older and a bit wiser higher priorities such as a growing family and demanding career take precedence over morbid thoughts like dying. In any event, death is always something that happens to somebody else, not you. Natural psychological protective mechanisms inhibit our thoughts of premature death unless it is suddenly staring us in the face. Even then we tend to keep such morose considerations at a distance by making light of them. In the film *Love and Death*, actress Diane Keaton says to Woody Allen, "I can't imagine anything worse than death." Replied Allen, "Oh, I don't know. Have you ever spent an hour with a life insurance salesman?"

Apart from being a morbid topic, life insurance to most people represents expense, not investment, and it is seen as an expense that will interfere with the accumulation of wealth. It's true you have to pay for life insurance. But if *you* don't, your beneficiaries and family will end up paying for your lack of foresight, perhaps for the rest of their lives.

If you do have to economize, consider cutting back on your other insurance policies and put the savings toward life insurance. For instance, you can make sure your home is not overinsured. If you are insuring your lot as well as your house, reduce the coverage and save on premiums. So far as your car is concerned, self-insure the fender-bender type of accident and put your premium money toward protecting yourself against a multi-million dollar liability suit (and toward life insurance). It will pay in the long run.

Remember where your priorities should be. Statistics Canada shows you where: every year one Canadian in every 140 dies; one automobile in every 187 registered is stolen; one in 358 dwellings is damaged by fire. One in every 7,500 dwellings is completely destroyed by fire.

Everything I write about life insurance applies as much to singles as to couples with or without children. In fact, I am often asked why young single people should spend money on insurance when they usually need every penny to get established on their own for the first time and to enjoy a life that is just starting to open up for them. There are 3 main reasons, and they all, like the planning process itself, relate to looking ahead and protecting yourself.

First, the younger you are when you buy insurance, the less the yearly premiums will cost. If you leave it too late, the cost could become prohibitive. Second, if you are insured, you are protected as long as you pay the premiums, even if you should become uninsurable a few years later for medical reasons. Third, death, unfortunately, is expensive in our society and becoming increasingly so. Regardless of who you are, you will leave behind costs related to funeral arrangements and possibly probate when you die. Somebody will have to pay these expenses. Perhaps your parents, for whom it might be a financial hardship. Even a small policy would take care of that problem.

I recall a graphic example. Years ago I visited a young man of 18 in British Columbia. Tommy Katt lived with his mother and older brother on a small seed farm in the Grand Forks Valley. The farm could not sustain them, so Tommy and his brother worked at full-time jobs elsewhere. Tommy was a construction laborer, blasting new highways through the mountainous interior of British Columbia. My visit with him lasted only 30 minutes. He had just come home from work filthy and exhausted and wanted to wash up because his mother had dinner on the table, so I told him quickly why I was there. His response startled me — it was the easiest sale I have ever made. He said, "You know, my brother Steve has a life insurance policy and I would like to get one too." We completed the application for $5,000 coverage and he went to his dinner. It carried a premium that I thought he could comfortably handle: $7.50 a month.

Five months later I received notice that Tommy's policy had lapsed because his premium check had bounced. Grand Forks was 120 miles away from my home base and I didn't think I could make the trip just to follow up Tommy's delinquency. Fortunately, my manager was going there the following week and during that visit he saw Tommy and reinstated the policy. I was pleased because when I learned it had lapsed, I wondered if I had done my job properly.

But I had misjudged Tommy. He was simply an abominable bookkeeper and he hadn't balanced his checkbook. He was quick to continue the policy when he was offered the chance.

Two months later Tommy's brother Steve phoned me. Early the previous morning, he said, Tommy and 4 or 5 others had been heading to a job site up the mountain. There had been a violent storm the night before and it had knocked down many trees and overhead lines. Some of these lines were lying across the narrow gravel road and Tommy jumped from the truck to move them out of the way. He didn't notice the live hydro line that had fallen among them; he took the full voltage and died on the spot.

His mother, who had no other money, used the proceeds of his policy to pay for the funeral expenses. The small balance she spent on something she had long wanted to do for herself: she moved with her few possessions to Alberta to live with a sister.

I've told many people in their 20s or 30s the story of Tommy Katt over the years and it often changes their attitudes. Life insurance is not just a morbid consideration for older, married people with children.

Okay, are you convinced that you should pay a bit more attention to life insurance? I hope so. And if you are, the first question you should ask yourself is "How much do I really need?"

Despite the plethora of information about life insurance that abounds, few people of my acquaintance know what they are doing or how much insurance they should have when it comes to buying it. And that includes many people selling it. Yet the salespeople are supposed to be experts. Experts are not infallible. A lot of salespeople have certain axes to grind and are limited to a certain line of policies. Others are inexperienced. Some are just not as capable as others. Mind you, there is not much new in that. I think it always has been a toss-up which expert you should believe, if any. Consider these opinions, as printed by the *Wall Street Journal* in 1985:

> *Everything that can be invented has been invented.*
> Charles H. Duell, director of the United States Patent Office, 1899;
>
> *Who the hell wants to hear actors talk?*
> Harry M. Warner, Warner Brothers Pictures, 1927;
>
> *Sensible and responsible women do not want to vote.*
> Grover Cleveland, 24th president of the USA, 1905;
>
> *There is no likelihood man can ever tap the power of the atom.*
> Robert Millikan, Nobel Prize in Physics, 1923;
>
> *Heavier than air machines are impossible.*
> Lord Kelvin, President of the Royal Society, about 1885;

> *[Babe] Ruth made a big mistake when he gave up pitching.*
> Tris Speaker, 1921.

Well, so much for experts. What follows is a simplified look at life insurance. This, after all, is a book about financial planning, not a definitive treatise on insurance. But I think I can help take some of the mystery out of life insurance, its need and uses, because, except for people like Agatha Christie, mystery doesn't pay.

How Much Should You Have?

On the simplest level, you use life insurance to replace your income, especially if you are a breadwinner, should you die prematurely or before you have had time to build up enough assets to do the job for you. In that respect life insurance is no different from fire insurance, which is designed to replace your house or contents if either burns. Or your car if it is stolen, damaged or totalled.

The main thing to keep in mind when deciding how much life insurance coverage you should have is to imagine your family's needs starting tomorrow, in case you should die in your sleep tonight.

On the most elemental level, how much coverage really means: what size of lump sum would your dependents need from the insurance company so when that sum is safely invested at a moderate return — say 10% — the resulting income each year would be sufficient to support them in reasonable fashion?

There are hundreds of rules-of-thumb, formulas, statistics, charts and tables purporting to indicate how much life insurance you should have. Most life insurance salespeople are well armed with them. And they can be useful, especially if you are trying to decide yourself how much coverage you need. See Figure 7 for one such chart. Universities have worked out unique formulas for the purpose. And I have already mentioned the rule-of-thumb of coverage: 10 times your annual income. (See Figure 8.)

HOW MUCH LIFE INSURANCE DO YOU NEED?

	Spouse's age:			
Your present earnings:	**25**	**35**	**45**	**55**
$ 15,000	$ 67,500	$ 97,500	$120,000	$105,000
23,500	152,000	188,000	199,500	176,500
30,000	225,000	240,000	255,000	210,000
40,000	300,000	320,000	320,000	280,000
65,000	487,000	487,500	487,500	421,500
75,000	562,000	562,500	562,500	499,500
90,000	675,000	675,000	675,000	585,000
110,000	825,000	825,000	825,000	715,000

Figure 7: This is one of many charts used in the industry to determine an individual's life insurance needs. The amount of insurance varies according to a spouse's age, government survivor benefits and life-expectancy.
(Source: Printed with permission of Vernon-Longman Publishing, inc.)

INCOME OBJECTIVES

Annual Gross Income	Percentage of Gross Income Required
Up to $35,000	70%
$35,001 to $39,000	66%
$39,001 to $43,000	63%
$43,001 to $48,000	60%
Over $48,000	57%

Figure 8: This is a simpler way of calculating life-insurance needs, according to a study done by a group of economists. The percentages are considered appropriate amounts that would allow a family to remain in its own world, so to speak, after the death of a wage-earner. It is assumed the mortgage is paid off (or a rent fund in place) and educational expenses are taken care of in some other way.
(Source: Printed with permission of Vernon-Longman Publishing, inc.)

CAPITAL / FAMILY NEEDS ANALYSIS

PRESENT VALUE OF LIQUID ASSETS		CURRENT LIABILITIES	
—Retirement Plan (Death Benefit)	______	—Final Expenses	______
—Other Life Insurance	______	—Home Mortgage	______
—Current Value of Vested Retirement Plan	______	—Emergency Fund	______
—Real Estate	______	—Educational Fund	______
—Stocks & Bonds	______	—Business Loans	______
—Mutual Funds	______	—Personal Loans	______
—Hard Assets	______	—Other Debts	______
—Business Interest	______		______
—Other Assets	______		______

SURVIVING FAMILY INCOME

	Dependency Period	Independent Period	Retirement
1. Spouse's estimated monthly income	______	______	______
2. Other Monthly Income	______	______	______
3. Desired Family Income	______	______	______

Figure 9: This chart is used in part to gather the figures needed to calculate the amount of life insurance or possible capital a family needs. From this an amount required to fund funeral expenses, pay off the mortgage, pay educational expenses and to provide an income for life, is deduced — to come from the capital supplied through insurance.

I believe very strongly, however, that the only formula that makes sense is to sit down with your family and work out specifically what life insurance they would need if the breadwinner or breadwinners died today. When I do this, I use what I call a *Capital/Family Needs Analysis* (Figure 9). A few terms used in this analysis (which includes a section called "Surviving Family Income" bear explanation:

- The general heading of "Present Value of Liquid Assets"

includes the assets that could be easily converted into cash if necessary to pay off debts or to provide income in the event of death. The seventh item, "Hard Assets," means investment-grade diamonds, gemstones, stamps, some rare coins, gold, silver, platinum. It does not include collectibles, such as personal jewelry.

- Under "Current Liabilities" the heading "Final Expenses" is the amount of money needed to cover death expenses — perhaps funeral and probate/surrogate court costs.
- "Emergency Fund" is just what it says: a family emergency fund of generally 3 to 6 months of after-tax income.
- "Educational Fund" will provide an education for the children in later years. Generally this is about $10,000 per child.
- We break down the 3 categories under the general heading of "Surviving Family Income" into 3 different periods. The "Dependency Period" is the time left until the youngest child is age 18. The "Independent Period" starts when the youngest child goes to college. We assume "Retirement" to start at age 65.
- "Spouse's Estimated Monthly Income" assumes the spouse is working or would work until retirement. "Other Monthly Income" means investment income or legacies. This might include child allowance and perhaps Canada Pension Plan or even widows' and orphans' benefits. I should say here that we don't mention these details in the analysis because our computer automatically includes them where appropriate throughout this analysis. If you were to do your own analysis, you would include all sources of income other than salary. The "Desired Family Income" is the total amount needed to keep the family together, living at home and in the style to which it has been accustomed.

The computer program that our company uses picks up the shortfall between the income from numbers 1 and 2 and the expenses estimated in number 3 in Figure 9. The computer does all the number-crunching and even factors in inflation. The amount of estimated inflation per year is agreed upon with the client, as is the possible increase in his or her investment yield with the passage of time. Generally we look at 10% return on investment to calculate income for the family.

You can see that our company's approach is not entirely do-it-yourself. We agree on a number of parameters with the client face-to-face, and let the computer do a lot of the work. The form would be a lot more complicated if we were going to list and calculate all the figures we need without the computer.

What Kind of Insurance Do You Need?

Besides protecting your dependents financially and yourself, in case your spouse should die, insurance can enable you to build up savings for retirement. That brings us to the point where you must determine what type of life insurance to buy.

In the insurance industry there are many confusing buzzwords describing what is essentially a simple product. To complicate matters even more there are self-styled experts who write columns and books about insurance. As often as not they are completely wrong in their understanding of the product.

There has always been a kind of mystique, and consequent confusion, surrounding the subject, and the marketing, of life insurance. That for many people has placed it in the well-I-guess-I'd-better-get-some-but-I'll-put-it-off-as-long-as-I-can category. There should be no esoteric, hidden or secret meaning about it, but insurance often is presented with so much attendant jargon that few fully understand what they are hearing and seeing.

In my seminars I often ask participants if they really understand the life insurance they already have. Invariably the answer is no. I ask if they understood what was told to them during the sales process. Most admitted that they could follow the logic while it was being presented, but the next day they were baffled when they tried to remember the details, and they could not repeat them. Frequently the presentation was accompanied by pages and pages and columns and columns of projections, extensions, statistics and terminology they didn't understand, references to "dividends" and "cash-surrender values" and "paid-up options." Even the non-buzzwords don't mean what they do in common usage. The "dividend" in life insurance isn't really a dividend as we usually understand it. A "premium" certainly isn't a premium as the word is commonly used. And goodness only knows what "non-forfeiture" or "reinstatements" mean. When you pile the confusing terminology on top of the dozens of different types of policies with fancy names and reams of options, it is little wonder why so few buyers understand what they have bought — and why many people shy away from buying anything.

There are three basic categories of life insurance: term, whole-life (sometimes called permanent, straight-life or ordinary-life), and universal (a recent entry in the insurance stakes).

Term: cheap and (relatively) simple. Term generally is the cheapest life insurance you can buy. Usually you are buying protection in the event of death only. There are variations and options in term policies. The most important options are those dealing with the periodic renewal of the policy (at a higher premium) and the conversion to a whole-life policy. You can buy a policy whose proceeds decline with time (decreasing-term) or which stay level (level-term). Most term policies have an eventual expiry date (perhaps age 70) though usually you can apply to renew even then. However, the premium is likely to be high, perhaps higher than whole-life by that time.

Most group insurance offered through your employer is term. In many cases the amount is not enough to cover your needs and the options may not be suitable. You will have to augment your group coverage with a policy you buy yourself or your coverage will be incomplete. And don't wait too long. Insurance premiums increase with your age. Also there is the chance you will become uninsurable, for medical reasons.

Whole-life: protection and savings. Whole-life insurance is in effect an enforced savings plan combined with protection. The premium you pay for a whole-life policy is considerably higher than that for a term policy offering the same amount of protection. Part of the difference in the premium is invested by the insurance company on the policyholder's behalf. Thus, a cash value builds up. The cash value is the amount the insurance company would return to you if you "cashed in" your policy and relieved them of any further obligations. If you don't cash in the policy, you can borrow against the cash value. Usually a whole-life policy is "paid-up" after a certain number of years, after which you pay no further premiums, but your protective coverage remains.

Your beneficiaries will always collect whatever coverage you paid for. But they do not get the cash value in addition — just the amount of protection you purchased. In fact, if you have borrowed against your policy's cash value and die before you have paid the debt off, the balance of what you owe will be deducted from the coverage before it is paid to your beneficiaries.

There are endless variations in options for whole-life insurance, most of them centering on different ways of dealing with the policy's cash value and ensuing "dividends." You should be able to find a whole-life policy and/or options that can be tailored to your specific requirements. That is a major plus for this form of life insurance.

Another plus is that your premium is the same throughout the time you pay it. In part this is a bit like equalized billing for your oil or gas furnace fuel — although you pay a bit more at the start of the policy (like summer fuel bills) you pay less near the end (like winter).

Don't automatically turn up your nose, like some people do, at the mention of using life insurance to save money. The enforced savings element of whole-life can be a lifesaver to those unsophisticated in the wondrous ways of investing savings. And since saving money is the crux of your financial plan, you can't afford not to consider all possibilities that help you save. Remember, your purpose in planning is eventual financial freedom. Or at least a comfortable retirement.

I recall once reading that the difference between an elderly gentleman and an old man is the amount of money each has. There is no question that money tends to bestow dignity upon some of those who have it. In the early 1960s, as a neophyte branch manager for my insurance company, I was learning my territory by calling on a few policyholders scattered around western Manitoba. The second call I made was to the owner of what appeared to be a very old policy, at least as far as I could tell from the policy number. His name was Ford and the address was a rural one a few miles out of Neepawa. I didn't plan to spend much time on the call because Mr. Ford was obviously a farmer and still busy with the harvesting.

As I approached the farm I spotted a combine in a nearby field, unloading wheat into a grain truck. I walked through the stubble to the middle-aged man operating the combine, introduced myself and explained I was there to review the policy of Mr. Ford. Was I talking with the right person? Ford was his name, all right, but the man I wanted was probably his father, who was just getting into the grain truck. The second Mr. Ford seemed to be older, so I knew I had my man. He nodded at me and we chatted. After a few moments he said, "You really don't want to talk to me. You want my father. He's back in the toolshed, over by the garage."

He cleared up my confusion before he drove off with the sweet-smelling, fresh-cut wheat. The first Mr. Ford was in his 50s and he operated the farm with the assistance of the driver, his father, who was in his 70s. The person I was seeking, my policyholder, was grandfather Ford, still active at 94.

I found the elderly gentleman in farmer's overalls and a railroad engineer's hat. He was tinkering at the workbench with a motor he had in a vise. We had a fascinating conversation.

Grandfather Ford had bought the policy in 1898. It was a 20-pay life so he hadn't paid any premiums since 1918 when the policy became paid up. He had never touched it. It was not large by today's standards, but it was all he had that was entirely his, so he had never used the policy's cash value. He had passed the farm along to his son, and his son had done the same with his son. Grandfather Ford's health was good and he could work at minor jobs. He still wanted to make himself useful and he was proud of his role around the farm. Possession of that whole-life policy meant a lot to him, too, partly because of its monetary value and partly because it meant he was still in a position to leave something to his family. He was not simply an old man living off the hard work of his son and grandson.

Grandfather Ford extended my visit a while with his reminiscences of the original settlement of the early West. His father had come from the United States, up the Red River to Winnipeg, to seek out a homestead of his own. He himself was born in 1867, right on that homestead and he had remained there all his 94 years.

He led me outside and to the top of a small knoll a hundred yards or so away. From the top he pointed out the distant highway — number 4, I think it was — still known locally by its original name of the Yellow Head Route. It begins in Winnipeg and is part of the Trans-Canada Highway until Portage La Prairie, where it branches off toward Saskatoon, Edmonton and the Yellow Head Pass through the Rockies. Grandfather Ford told me that when he was a young man he used to sit on that knoll and listen to the Red River cart trains stridently rasping their way toward Saskatoon and Edmonton. The Yellow Head track passed by the farm almost a mile away but, he said, you could hear the heavily laden, wooden oxcarts from miles away, carry hopeful settlers and all their worldly goods towards a new life. Though their axles and wheels were greased periodically with animal fat, the excessive dust of the trail still made them squeal unmercifully most of the time.

It was to accommodate those caravans, Grandfather Ford told me, that the main streets in the big prairie cities today are so wide. Portage Avenue in Winnipeg is a case in point as are some thoroughfares in Saskatoon and Edmonton, all streets that follow the path of the Yellow Head. The oxcarts traveled 10 abreast because otherwise the stupendously thick layer of dust covering the trail would suffocate both oxen and settlers just 2 or 3 back if they had moved in single file. Besides, the Prairie land was so flat it didn't much matter where you traveled or how much room you took.

Grandfather Ford's foresight in purchasing a whole-life policy almost three-quarters of a century before gave him the peace of mind to know that when he died he would not be a burden on his family. The old gentleman's attitude and reminiscences left me profoundly grateful I had made that otherwise uneventful trip through the hinterlands of Manitoba.

Whether you should buy whole-life like Grandfather Ford or sometimes less expensive term insurance is a contentious issue inside and outside the insurance industry. Proponents of term-only insurance claim that you yourself could do a much better job than an insurance company of investing that extra and substantial portion of premium that does not apply to protection, especially inside a tax-sheltered RRSP. And you might, if you have the self-discipline and the cash to do so. It is partly to answer that specific criticism of whole-life that insurance companies in the last few years have introduced a different form of coverage called universal life insurance.

Universal: the best of both worlds? Universal-life insurance is a form of whole-life that offers the buyer some choice of how the extra premium is invested. This means the return can fluctuate with the market (though it is usually guaranteed not to fall below a certain level). Because the company does not guarantee a fixed rate, the premiums can be lower than whole-life, though usually still more than for term, unless you opt for no investment component. It is flexible in that you can vary how much you choose to put into the investment component, and you can change the type of investment vehicle at little or no cost if you see the general investment climate changing. You can even use some of the "profits" from your investment to add to the protection side of the policy.

Here are a few things to keep in mind when buying life insurance:

- Regardless of what type of insurance you buy, remember that buying the right amount for your needs is your prime consideration.
- The only good life insurance is the insurance that is in force the day you die.
- In order to get the amount of insurance they need, most young people can only afford term. That's fine. But keep in mind that term premiums generally increase with the years, to the point that they might well become unaffordable. Also make sure you buy the renewable option. That means if you buy 5-year term you have the right to renew your coverage for a further 5 years at the end of each 5-year period, without any evidence of insurability (no medical). The right to renew is yours, not the company's.
- If you buy term insurance, make sure it is convertible. This option allows you to convert part or all of your term insurance to a whole-life policy from your insurer. That means you should deal with a company that has a good portfolio of whole-life or permanent plans so that if you ever want to convert you have a good range of suitable products to choose from. Quite often smaller companies will have extremely good term policies and rates but you'll find that they don't have an attractive assortment of whole-life products available. Some companies like to offer term almost like a "loss leader" to attract initial business which they later hope to convert to whole-life plans which may not be as cost-effective for you. Keep in mind that price shouldn't always be the most important factor even when you buy term insurance.
- Convertibility is important enough to rate a second mention here. The purpose of financial planning is to enable you to become self-insured and independent by the time you are 65 or earlier, depending on your goals. (Self-insured means you don't need to have insurance because you have enough money to take care of yourself and your dependents in any emergency.) That's good in theory, but in my experience I have seldom seen clients' needs for some life insurance completely disappear even upon retirement. For instance, at death considerable expenses mount up. And certainly taxes will have to be paid. Quite often there are still people financially dependent on breadwinners. This means you never really know

whether you will need whole-life insurance until later in life. To keep the option to whole-life open, it is worth the small amount extra in term premiums for the conversion feature.

- You should review your insurance coverage at least every year. Your circumstances change and inflation is always with us. What might be adequate protection now could become inadequate in even one year's time. As an example take inflation alone: if inflation is 5% (a modest assumption these days) and if you don't review your insurance portfolio for 5 years, the amount of your protection has decreased 25% in that period. You may have improved your lifestyle during those years, added to your family, bought a cottage — any number of circumstances that would increase, not decrease your dependents' need for life insurance. An annual review is pretty important.
- Shop the market. Not all life-insurance companies have the same approach or products. No one company will necessarily offer the best product available on the market in each of their various product lines. It is important to compare. This is where a good financial planner can help you save shoe leather and telephone ear. A planner who is not locked into a single line of products (and there are some) can, through the computer, analyze a great number of different insurance companies' products to determine which is the best for you.
- Finally, insurance for both spouses in a family is absolutely essential. It doesn't matter that one spouse might not be earning wages outside the house. If you haven't worked it out before, you'd be surprised if not horrified by how much it would cost to replace the services of the spouse who stays at home to run the household, especially if younger children are involved. You'd need a nurse, a babysitter, a cook, a cleaner, a gardener, a launderer, a chauffeur, a host or hostess and on and on and on. To hire all of these people would cost more than most breadwinners are earning. However, to be practical, assuming a single housekeeper could be found to do the job, for the next 10 to 15 years, you'd need insurance coverage in the neighborhood of $200,000 on the stay-at-home spouse.

You might feel the cost a bit excessive, especially if you calculate you need about $300,000 coverage yourself. You can solve the problem, however, by acquiring a joint-life policy.

> This would provide $200,000 should the household spouse die or $300,000 if the breadwinner dies. And the total cost is little more than the cost of covering just one life.

There are innumerable uses for life insurance beyond your individual need for protection or a savings program. Life insurance is one of the most imaginative financial-planning tools ever created. There is no other way you can create an estate with a stroke of a pen and for so little cost. And it has a variety of irreplaceable uses in the business world. It is a shame that the life-insurance industry and its products are so often misunderstood and abused to the extent that they are. Be that as it may, if you are to develop an effective personal financial plan, life insurance is an essential part of the plan's foundation. So, get the best advice you can and forge ahead.

Disability: The Crippling Facts

- 1 in 8 Canadians is disabled to some degree, according to Statistics Canada.
- The probability that you will suffer a disability before age 40 is more than 2 to 1 compared to the chances of dying before that age.
- The chances of a 30-year-old man becoming disabled for a prolonged period of time prior to age 65 is 1 out of 3. In fact, the risk of disability before age 65 is 50% greater than the risk of death.
- 1 in 5 Canadian adults was involved in some kind of accident in 1987. As a point of reference, only 1 in 140 Canadians died in 1987.
- If you are 45 years old, the chances of your becoming disabled during the next 15 years are 1 in 4. Your chances of dying during the next decade and a half are 7 to 1.
- A government agency study in the United States has found that death caused 3% of all mortgage foreclosures, but disability caused 48%.
- There are 70,000 wheelchair-users in Canada and 10,000 new chairs are sold every year.
- Despite a very restrictive Canada Pension Plan disability clause, some 94,000 people are collecting benefits under it.
- More than 300,000 Canadians suffer from Alzheimer's disease.
- A new diabetic is diagnosed every 50 seconds in Canada.
- Almost ½ of all Canadian males and more than ½ of all

females have at least one health problem.

- Disability in the technical sense means you will be incapable of working for a minimum of almost 3 months. And if you are disabled for at least 90 days, you will be that way for 5.4 years, the statistical average indicates.

Are your eyes starting to glaze over from a surfeit of statistics? Well, prop them open. Get a cup of coffee and keep reading — you can't afford not to. If you are like most people, it's no work — no money!

The facts are simple and clear. If you don't protect yourself adequately, the odds are that you will become disabled at some time or other, and that could lead to premature, and permanent, poverty.

Even if you have developed an emergency fund, you could still be in trouble. One year of disability (with no income) could wipe out 10 years of savings, even if you had put away as much as 10% of your income every year. A lengthy disability literally could decimate a lifetime of savings.

And don't automatically assume that you are adequately covered through your benefits package at work. You likely will find on close examination that that coverage isn't enough. If you are self-employed, you should increase your coverage to keep pace with an increasing income.

Take a look at Figure 10. It charts your chances of becoming disabled (or dying) before you have paid off a mortgage.

DISABILITY: A FACTOR TO BE CONSIDERED

Age	Chance of Death Within 15 Years	Chance of Disability Within 15 Years	Chance of Death Within 30 Years	Chance of Disability Within 30 Years
20	1 in 35	1 in 10	1 in 10	1 in 3
25	1 in 29	1 in 8	1 in 8	1 in 3
30	1 in 22	1 in 6	1 in 5	1 in 3
35	1 in 15	1 in 5	1 in 4	1 in 2
40	1 in 10	1 in 4	1 in 3	1 in 2
45	1 in 7	1 in 4	1 in 2	1 in 2
50	1 in 4	1 in 4	Almost certain	Almost certain

Figure 10: The chance of your becoming seriously disabled is significantly greater than your chance of dying. You can't afford to ignore this risk, especially when it's easy to protect yourself and your family through disability insurance.
(Source: Printed with permission of Vernon-Longman Publishing, inc.)

Living Longer Has Its Problems

Why are these statistics on disability so staggering — much more monstrous in magnitude than life-expectancy figures? And, in fact, on the rise? According to an organization that conducts nationwide health surveys, the number of individuals permanently disabled by disease jumped sharply in the 1970s. During that decade the population grew 10% but at the same time the number of disabled rose 37%. The diseases most responsible for the increase included high blood pressure, diabetes, heart disease, cancer and muscle and bone disorders.

I doubt that these diseases are more prevalent today than in the past. But thanks to modern medicine and its continually evolving techniques, people are living longer. In the past many would have died if they contracted these diseases. Now they survive, but in many cases contribute to disability statistics. The same is true of accident victims.

Until recent years, the industry's spotlight has been directed steadfastly on life insurance. However, attention now is focusing more and more on how disability affects the financial life of the individual or family. I can think of a number of reasons for the late arrival of disability on the scene. For one thing, disability insurance is tremendously more complicated than life insurance. Death is final, incontrovertible and inevitable. In a way it is easier to understand than disability. Disability usually is not terminal and it comes in many forms and degrees. In any event, accidents will happen, but they always happen to our neighbors, right? Never to ourselves.

Whatever the reason, be thankful disability insurance is available. It is another necessary cornerstone in the foundation of your personal financial plan.

Even the Master Can Learn from the Novice

I have always felt that if you want to learn, you must become a teacher. Early in my career I taught grades 9 and 10 algebra and geometry. I found that through teaching I learned more about the subject than I did in the years I studied it as a student. To teach something well and to communicate that knowledge to students, you really have to have a good grasp of the subject-matter. You don't get that grasp by using simply memory or rote; you must understand the subject's principles, theories and practical applications in order to translate them to students.

As a young pilot officer in the Royal Canadian Air Force I was ordered to teach navigation to air cadets. When I started, I knew a little about spherical trigonometry, which is the basis of navigation, but I didn't know much about navigation. I learned very quickly, however, because I had to keep one step ahead of my students. More than once I learned from them because of their questioning, sharp minds.

The same thing happened a few years ago when I was conducting a class on disability insurance in one of my many training seminars for my company's own financial-planning center presidents and account executives. I used an overhead projector with plenty of charts and statistics. That, plus the material in our workbooks and my definitive explanations were pretty impressive, I thought, and got the essence of the subject across effectively.

The class and I discussed how best to convey all the complicated facts to my clients. It's one thing for account executives — considered experts in the subject — to have all this information at their fingertips. It's quite another for them to effectively communicate to clients about the need to include disability insurance in their financial scheme of things.

At one point I suggested to the class that a key to the clients' understanding of disability protection is to convince them that after a disability their expenses tend to increase at the same time that their income dries up. They still have all their normal fixed expenses — they have to eat, pay their rent or mortgages, buy clothing and keep up with their car payments. But, at the same time, additional costs pop up that they might never have considered. You might have to have your car fitted with hand controls. Also, it could cost a packet to renovate your home to accommodate a wheelchair. You might have to rent or buy special beds, walkers and various therapeutic equipment. If you are hospitalized for a long period there can be additional costs to make your hospital stay comfortable. If you require specialized treatment at a location far from home, you might be burdened by extra costs for transportation for yourself or your family.

The class and I agreed that in most cases the cost of a prolonged disability is even greater than that of death. It may be morbid but there's little question that you could become a financial liability to your family rather than an asset, if you aren't properly prepared to deal with the uncertain consequences of unexpected illness or accident.

After the class had listened attentively to all I had to say about disability, one of the students spoke up.

"Well, Grant, you've given us a mountain of facts and figures. But that much information can be confusing to some people. I'd like to show you how I get the need across to my clients in a simpler way. May I use the blackboard?"

He went to the board and drew a large triangle, like a pyramid. He divided it with 3 horizontal lines, the same distance apart, into 4 layers. In the smallest at the top he wrote the figure $1,500. In the next, slightly larger, segment he wrote $15,000. In the second-from-the-bottom one he wrote $150,000. And in the bottom segment, $1,500,000.

"Suppose you had these 4 assets in your possession," he said to the class. "Each asset is worth 10 times more than the one above.

"Now suppose you wanted to insure these assets against loss, and you had only a certain amount of money to do it. Let's say you have only $1,000 available.

"What portion of that $1,000 would you use to insure the asset at the top, the $1,500 asset? And what portion would you use to insure the last item on the triangle, the $1,500,000 asset?"

Well, the class looked at his pyramid for a moment and collectively agreed that it was obvious that they would spend a lot more of their $1,000 to insure the most valuable, $1,500,000 asset. They would insure the other assets relative to their values, with little or no money going toward the $1,500 asset.

"You know, it's odd," he said to the class. "What you've said clearly makes sense. But the way most people apply their insurance dollars usually is in the reverse order. They tend to spend most money on their less-valuable assets.

"Let me explain that. Supposing the $1,500 section of the triangle represents the value of your television set and VCR. How many here today have these devices insured for their full value, which means replacement value with a low deductible and insured against all eventualities such as fire, theft, burglary and so on?"

Almost everybody in the room put up their hands.

"Now let's assume the $15,000 asset represents your car. How many have their cars insured?" Naturally all hands again went up in agreement. Then he added, "And chances are your coverage includes low deductible and again protection against all possible claims.

"Let's assume that the $150,000 asset on the pyramid represents the value of your home. How many people have your home insured?" Again, all the hands went up.

And he added, "I'm sure that you have insured it against every possible contingency, right up to the replacement value, right?

"Well, let's go further. Let's assume the $1,500,000 asset at the base of the triangle represents your earning potential for the balance of your life. How many of you have $1,500,000 of disability income insurance?"

After a few quiet moments just a few hands went up. Maybe everybody hesitated because they had to figure out in their heads how much insurance they did have. That would be typical. Most people have never worked out how much money would be coming in if they should become disabled.

My student's illustration was dramatic and designed to draw attention to the value of potentially lost income. Mind you, you don't have to cover a face value of $1.5 million to be properly insured. But you do have to have enough so that the insurance payments you receive during your lifetime would add up to what you could lose in that same period.

There Are a Lot of Variables When It Comes to Disability

That brings us to the main difficulty of understanding and dealing with disability insurance, compared to life insurance: there are so many variables when it comes to disability. What, for instance, do we mean by disability? Is it total or partial? How long might you be considered medically disabled? Were you disabled because of an accident or sickness? On or off the job? Who might be responsible for paying — the government through unemployment insurance? Or Workers' Compensation? Or possibly a negligent employer? Or a driver? There are a lot of difficult questions; each of which might have different answers or different nuances in answers.

It is considerably easier to figure out how much your beneficiaries would collect in the event of your death. Death is pretty conclusive.

Either you are or you aren't. An insurance company will act on a death certificate. The amount you are covered for usually is pretty well defined and determined in advance. There are far fewer shades and gray areas in life insurance compared to disability.

To give you an example, $2,000 of disability insurance might cost you anywhere from $5 to $500 a month. The wide discrepancy in premiums depends on the conditions under which the $2,000 would be paid.

For instance, a surgeon might arrange coverage of $2,000 a month, payable for the rest of a lifetime, in the event that he or she lost the fingertips from one finger and could no longer operate. The payments might continue even though he or she might retrain as a radiologist and earn twice as much money. Perhaps the $2,000 might even be indexed to the rate of inflation. This kind of coverage could be considered a Cadillac, or perhaps these days, a Mercedes-Benz benefit. It might cost around $500 a month in premiums for that quality of plan.

If, on the other hand, the same $2,000 were to be paid only if the surgeon were injured while traveling after 8:00 p.m. on public transit, then a $5-per-month premium might be appropriate because the chances of collecting it are very, very slim. In other words, it's not just the amount of coverage that determines the cost. The combination of conditions that dictate the likelihood of collecting has a great bearing too.

This last example is a little extreme, like the old insurance-industry joke: your spouse would collect a fortune if you should be trampled by a herd of wild elephants on a Sunday afternoon on Main Street on a snowy day in July. But you get the idea: disability insurance can become fairly complicated because there can be so many ands, ifs or buts written into the contract.

How Much Disability Insurance Do You Need?

Let me describe the procedure I would use to help you, assuming you were my client, calculate how much and what kind of disability insurance you need. You could do this yourself.

The first step is to determine the amount of coverage. We work up your cash-flow statement and determine your fixed expenses. These expenses will continue even though you become disabled. We use

Figure 3 from Chapter 6 to record the raw data. Next we ascertain how much extra money might be required in the event of disability. This list would include:

- How much you should continue to save. If you have children, you still want to educate them and if you are employed full-time, you will still want to retire at some date in the future. You have to save for this so you must allow for these costs when determining disability insurance needs.
- Other costs related to disability. If you were confined to a wheelchair you might have to modify your home accordingly. This could mean changes to sidewalks and stairs, the bathroom or kitchen and perhaps the installation of an elevator.
- Your transportation costs could increase substantially, especially if you have to equip your car with hand controls.
- You might require special beds, drugs and other medical paraphernalia. You might need home-care nursing and this might not be available under your current insurance programs. You have to be realistic about what might happen and allow for the worst scenario in your calculations.

I would help you tote up the possible benefits you might already qualify for if you become disabled and evaluate them. There are, for instance, a plethora of government and employer benefits you might have.

- If you contribute to the Canada or Quebec pension plans, you may qualify for disability income benefits, which, late in 1989, paid up to a maximum of $681.23 per month. Additional benefits are available to you if you have dependent children. You don't automatically qualify for the maximum; the amount depends on how much income you have earned and whether or not you have contributed the maximum into the government plan.

  The question arises also as to whether you can collect. It is generally conceded that the Canada and Quebec plans contain fairly restrictive definitions as to what constitutes disability. If you do collect, you will do so until you reach age 65 or until recovery. And the benefits are indexed.

- You may be covered for disability under Unemployment Insurance, but generally these benefits span only short-term disabilities, perhaps 15 weeks. And they start only after a 2-week waiting period. Other restrictions also apply.
- You could collect benefits from the Workers' Compensation Board if you were hurt on the job. This might amount to as much as 90% of your net average earnings, to a maximum of $12,722 a year.
- Your automobile insurance policy might provide some coverage, depending on the province in which you live. Generally the payouts are small and of limited duration.
- Most people tend to rely on their group income-replacement benefits at work. There are usually 2 types of benefits: one is short-term and might cover you for the first 13 weeks of a disability, perhaps even up to 26 weeks. These plans tend to pay from the first day of an accident or the 8th day of an illness.

  Your group plan might contain a long-term coverage. This would start where the short-term plan ends. Often there is a 3-or 6-month elimination period, which means it starts paying you only after that period. The coverage usually ranges from 50% to 75% of your gross income and it is integrated with Unemployment Insurance and Canada Pension Plan benefits. (This means the plan will top up the payments from these other plans to the agreed percentage of your gross — you can't add them all together.) Sometimes a group plan will impose an absolute dollar ceiling. So if you are an above-average wage-earner, chances are that your maximum benefit will be less than the 50% or 75% level.

Group disability coverage is good to have. Sometimes, however, an employer might replace the group plan with less-attractive coverage. Of course, if you leave your firm, you also leave your benefits behind. In any event, benefits stop at age 65.

I would help you check the definition of disability in your group policy. Some are more restrictive than others, and you should know exactly what you could expect. You also should find out what happens if you are disabled for a while, then go back to work, and then become disabled again from the same cause. Different plans specify various conditions under which they will not pay.

Compare the cost of your group plan. To most of us, group implies low cost, but this is not always so. There are cases where a large number of older employees in the benefits pool of a company could inflate the average cost of a group plan to more than it would cost you to buy a personally tailored individual plan.

It has been my experience that clients usually find the benefits offered by their group plan probably won't be adequate to meet all their needs. This is especially true for upper-level management since group plans are designed for the average or lower-than-average earner. And they tend to be structured so that if you become disabled, it will be economically difficult for you to stay off the job indefinitely. Their limitations are an inducement to get you back to work as soon as possible, which is not always medically wise.

There are other types of disability (and accident) plans available on a mail-order basis or through charge (credit) cards. Generally these plans are pretty restrictive so far as the amount and conditions of payment are concerned. To collect from some of them you have to be hospitalized. Some pay for only a certain contractual repayment cost such as your credit-card or mortgage-loan balances but not necessarily the entire balance.

Questions to Ask About Disability Plans

So what do you do about all this? You buy some individual disability income protection from one of a variety of supplier companies. The amount you buy depends on the amount of other coverage you have and the conditions it contains. You will have to do some homework to obtain all the facts from various sources and then blend what you need together. If you decide to do it yourself and not use the services of a disability-insurance expert (not life, but disability), then here are a few questions you should ask:

- What is the insurer's definition of disability?
- Can you collect if you are only partially disabled, or must you be totally disabled?
- What happens if the disability recurs?
- Are the policy's benefits indexed to some cost-of-living factor? If not, your benefits might no longer be enough to provide adequate income after 3 or 4 years of inflation.
- Does the policy cover *all* types of accidents and sickness, and

does it contain restrictions with respect to pre-existing health conditions?

- How many days (or months) do you have to be disabled before benefits start? And when are the actual payments made? Are they paid 1 or 2 months in arrears?
- How often do you have to submit evidence of continuing disability in order to keep collecting payments?
- Does the contract allow you to work part time — or any time — and still collect benefits?
- Will the policy pay benefits if the Canada Pension Plan does not, or if you are getting Workers' Compensation or Unemployment Insurance benefits?
- Are there any exclusions, such as self-inflicted injuries, acts of war or pregnancy? How would they affect you?
- What are the terms of the contract? Is it a guaranteed renewable or perhaps a non-cancelable policy? Simply put, *non-cancelable* means that the insurance company cannot cancel the policy and it cannot increase the premiums. *Guaranteed renewable* means that the company cannot refuse to renew your policy, but it can change the premiums for various classes of people within the plan if the statistics within those classes change from year to year.

How Long Do You Wait? How Long Do You Collect?

The first conditions to check thoroughly about a prospective disability policy are the elimination and the benefit periods. Elimination is the length of time you have to pay your own costs (perhaps the first 30, 60, 90 or 180 days or even 1 year) before the benefits kick in. It's a bit like the deductible amount in car insurance. Obviously the longer the elimination period, the lower your premium cost, other things being equal.

The benefit period spells out how long you can collect disability income under the polcy if you become sick or injured. A benefit period could be for 5 years, 10 years or to age 65. The longer the benefit period, the higher the premium.

Generally speaking, you should contract for a policy with a lengthy elimination period. Just as a high deductible lowers the cost of car insurance, a longer elimination period reduces the cost of disability coverage. This is an ideal use for your personal emergency fund that I mentioned earlier: it should carry you through the elimination period until the benefits start.

Once you do start collecting, make sure that you can do so right up to age 65. And that the payments are boosted by cost-of-living adjustments along the way. Remember, you are trying to use disability insurance to protect yourself (and any dependents) against a major catastrophe — that means long-term disability. You should be able to take care of the short-term problems yourself from your emergency fund.

Some Outside Help

How do you pick your way safely through the minefield of benefits, clauses, conditions and terms, to say nothing of the performance of various insurers? Because disability insurance is so complicated, I suggest that you rely on outside expertise. You should look for a person who represents a good-quality company or companies, and who has experience insuring disability.

As a layperson how will you know whom to choose? For one thing, check your expert's professional designations and degrees. For instance, if the person comes from the life-insurance industry does he or she have the qualifications of both experience and professional CLU designations? Agents who specialize in disability coverage usually have attained the Registered Health Underwriters (RHU) designation. The Chartered Financial Planner (CFP) designation indicates the holder is conversant with a wide range of insurance- and financial-sector products, including disability income plans. The Registered Financial Planner (RFP) has passed examinations covering the entire field of financial planning and has gained some experience in the field, too.

It is important also to deal with companies well recognized in the industry for offering good-quality disability-income products. There are companies that specialize in and have a high profile in the disability field. But there are many first-line life-insurance companies that offer disability-income products along with their life plans. These are highly regarded as well. Ask around, especially of people whose judgment you respect. It doesn't take long to discover what companies and products are well regarded. If you haven't time, call in a financial-planning organization, so long as the individual you deal with is well qualified.

15

Putting It All Together

The structure of a personal financial plan is relatively simple. It consists of a basic 6-step process:

1. Establishing your current situation
2. Establishing where you want to be, down the road
3. Evaluating what you need to do to get there
4. Putting it all on paper
5. Bringing the paper plan to life
6. Keeping track of how you're doing (and altering course from time to time, as necessary)

You can put a plan together yourself, or you can seek professional help from a qualified financial planner. I recommend you use an expert's brains and experience to help you, and I say that not just because it is in my own interest that you do so. In the course of your planning you will eventually run into some financial aspects requiring specialized knowledge — for example, tax or pension legislation — to say nothing of countless hours of repetitive calculations you'll have to do.

If you use outside help (and it won't necessarily cost you anything to do so) you could have the planner do the whole job. Or you could complete most of the plan yourself and then call on a planner to put the finishing touches to it. Whichever way you choose, you are an integral part of the process yourself. Even the cleverest planner can't do the job without your input.

Additional help is available from other sources: educational seminars in communities across Canada; self-help books; newspapers and magazines, some of which are devoted to helping readers with money management and personal financial planning.

Why Is Financial Planning Suddenly So Popular? Because of the computer, that's why. And more specifically, the microcomputer. Until only a decade or so ago access to professional financial planning lay exclusively in the domain of the well-to-do or the highly paid executive. Only they could afford the services of the phalanx of expensive technical advisors needed to put a plan together. A good tax accountant, a life underwriter, a health underwriter, a mutual-funds expert, a tax- and estate-planning specialist, a trust company officer, a bank advisor — these were just some of the specialists needed. And certainly you would also need a mathematician or an actuary or both to work long hours into the night, day after day, to handle all the calculations, permutations and combinations a client would want to see in a financial plan.

But the miracle of the microchip has allowed us to stuff all that expertise into a computer small enough to hold on your lap. What used to be a million-dollar facility filling an entire room now resides in a little box, at a fraction of the price. If the cost of cars had evolved the same way as computer capability you would now be able to buy a Rolls-Royce for a couple of dollars rather than $200,000.

That little lap-top or desktop micro with its millisecond speed and megabyte storage capacity has made financial planning affordable for middle-income Canadians. Much of financial planning is bringing together the multitude of variable calculations required so clients can look at options that allow them to make sensible choices. Let's look at the 6 steps I listed above in more detail and you will see better why the computer has made it all possible.

1. Establishing Your Current Situation

In other words, get the facts about the exact state of your finances today. You can't move toward anything if you don't know where you're starting from. The first step is to work out a balance sheet, which is a statement of your net worth (see Figure 4, Chapter 6). This means listing and totaling up all the things you own, then subtracting from that total the list of what you owe. The result is your net worth. You may be pleasantly surprised to find you are worth more than you thought.

Then you work out your cash flow statement. I don't mean a budget, but rather where your money is going to and where it is coming from. More correctly I should say, perhaps, where your money is not going to. The cash flow statement (see Figure 3, Chapter 6) summarizes your income and your expenses on an average monthly basis. What you have left (if anything) is what you use to achieve the financial goals and plans that you will develop in step 2, below.

The computer stores this information so you can pull it out and use it — even change it — during the other planning stages. This makes the successive planning steps infinitely easier.

2. Establishing Where You Want to Be, Down the Road

A subtitle for this step might be: "Goal Setting." A financial plan only makes sense in the context of the goals that you establish today. These set out where you want to be, or what you want to do, in the years ahead. There are a number of rules-of-thumb, perhaps a few "ought tos," and various formulas for financial success floating around the planning industry and taken by some practitioners as gospel. But ultimately it is your goals, and your goals alone, that determine what has to be done, not what somebody else tells you. What is important to you should be the decisive factor in shaping your future.

Individuals' financial planning goals can vary widely depending on ambitions, lifestyles, priorities. If you have a spouse or partner, it is essential that the goals developed and used in the financial plan be mutual ones. Ay, and there's the rub only too often. Agreeing on goals, especially retirement ones, is frequently the single most difficult step in planning, for you, your partner, and the planner who might be helping you orchestrate a harmonious financial composition. You'd be surprised at the discords in couples' outlooks when they are faced with setting down their goals on paper. Even couples who have been together a long time. They think they know each other and that they share similar values. But often they never have addressed some of the questions put to them by the planner. Agreeing on goals can take a lot of soul-searching from couples. But it has to be done.

There are a lot of questions you must ask yourself when setting goals. Also, you should recognize there is no right or wrong about long-term goals of retirement or financial independence. What does financial independence actually mean to you? And by what age? Do you want to be a multimillionaire, a millionaire or is being "comfortable" enough?

Do you have particular employment goals? Do you want to become self-employed or do you intend to work for your present employer until retirement? Do you have a yen to work after age 65 or 70?

Education should be an important element in a family's thinking. For instance, what kind do you want for your children, and how much do you want to contribute toward it? Do you feel you should pay all the cost, or just a portion? Do your ambitions for your kids extend to a doctoral degree at an Ivy League college or a certificate from a community college? There is no right or wrong answer. It all depends on what you want to make available to your children.

How much life insurance should you have and how much disability income do you require? Consider here your particular goals and what you want for yourself and your dependents in the event of unexpected disaster.

How big an emergency or opportunity fund do you want to build up? What are your investment goals? What do you feel is an acceptable rate of return on your assets? What is your risk tolerance — do you seek or avoid risk and to what degree? What is your opinion as to the rate of inflation for the next decade or two? Figure 11, in Chapter 17, shows the questionnaire I recommend you use to help determine your risk tolerance. You must answer all these questions and more to be able to determine the type of investments and the consequent yields that you can expect.

The great thing about the computer is that you can set up a series of goals, plug them into the computer and the machine will develop a scenario. If it doesn't look quite right, you can adjust goals or assumptions quickly and the machine will spew out different scenarios. You can go through this "what if" routine a number of times until you get it right. What would the results be if my investments were to yield 12% rather than 10%? What would my plan look like if inflation was 5% rather than 6%, or the prime rate 16% instead of 12%? Years ago you'd have needed a battery of mathematicians and actuaries working round the clock to make all the calculations and all the recalculations when you altered assumptions. And yet again if you wanted another change. The computer now does it in seconds.

3. Evaluating What You Need to Do to Get There

Once you have determined where you are starting from and what your goals are, the computer plugs in all the variations of Canada Pension Plan, Unemployment Insurance and the like and determines whether you have the assets and/or the income to achieve the goals you have established. Whether you do or you don't, you now must develop a plan for overcoming any shortfall or for using efficiently the extra income you have. Again the computer is extremely useful here to make a variety of calculations based on a number of assumptions. You can change interest-rate (or other) assumptions throughout the plan or segments of it until the results are comfortable. You massage the figures and approaches until you get one that works for you.

4. Putting It All on Paper

Every good financial plan should be on paper. The document should contain all the computer printouts (or hand calculations) such as net worth and cash flow statements and capital-needs analysis and so on. It must outline all your goals and what you need to do to achieve them, along with special areas that require your attention. This enables you to come up with a checklist of those items that should be looked after so that you can start to set priorities.

Chances are you are not going to be able to achieve everything you want immediately. It's going to take time, and it is a continuous, ongoing process. Putting it all on paper helps to focus what you need to do more sharply, and it gives you something tangible to check against from time to time to see if you are on track.

The appendix at the end of this book contains a summary and various excerpts from an actual financial plan to give you an idea of what a real plan should look like. The names have been changed to protect the innocent.

5. Bringing the Paper Plan to Life

It goes without saying that a plan is of no value unless it is implemented. If you don't bring your plan to life, it would be like commissioning an architect to provide you with beautiful sketches and a complete set of working drawings of your dream home, and then failing to hire a general contractor to get on with the job of building.

Your written plan contains all the financial elements in your life, along with priorities and recommended action. It allows you to make thoughtful decisions. The recommendations of the financial planner (or yourself, if you undertake the planning alone) should be clear-cut and concise so you will know in advance the cause and effect of the actions you are called upon to take.

Alas, the breath of life is breathed upon too few plans. It is somewhat ironic, even sad, to learn that many people who have gone to the trouble of having plans developed for them do not follow up. The conventional wisdom (and I have no hard facts to back this up) floating around the financial-planning industry says that about 80% of all the financial plans done for a flat fee are never fully implemented. This seems like a very high percentage and you might well wonder why otherwise sane, rational, normal people wouldn't follow up with something so important to their long-term well-being. I think there are three main reasons:

- The first is the same reason most of us didn't get a faster start on our savings programs, or do an adequate job assessing what life insurance we needed in the early stages. We simply get caught up with the priorities and cares of everyday life. The long term takes a back seat.

  For instance, a typical financial plan might call for a reduction in your mortgage principal by increasing monthly payments. It may also suggest buying some more life-insurance protection, and perhaps rearranging some of the assets in your estate to free up money for investments. It's not unusual for a planner to make 8 to 10 recommendations that you have to decide to do. When all that is added onto the basic problems of everyday survival, it can seem to be almost too much to think about. And when life closes in around you with so many demands you might do just that, think about it for a while. Without acting.

- The second reason involves the phenomenon of change. Implementing a financial plan almost inevitably requires change. And most people, me included, don't really like to make changes, particularly if we are comfortable with our current bad habits. If it involves change, you are likely to create 1,001 reasons to delay plan implementation.

  Maybe your mortgage is up for renewal next year and you really don't want to start paying down the principal until you find out the level of interest rates you are going to have to pay next year. So, you postpone that decision.

  Perhaps you need more life insurance. But that might mean a medical and you would rather avoid examining your state of health. You put it off (especially if you are like Woody Allen and don't want to spend an hour with an insurance salesperson).

  Maybe your plan calls for making a will. What could be more morbid, you imagine? Besides, you have to phone your lawyer for an appointment (probably for 2 months from now), and it is going to cost money, and there never seems to be a convenient time to get you and the lawyer together, and . . . Result: procrastination.

  Perhaps your plan contains a recommendation to convert some of your spare cash into savings. But that would mean tightening your belt a bit and perhaps curtailing this year's holiday plans. And you really need a good vacation to recharge the batteries.

  Really, the best idea is to put off starting to implement the whole plan until after Christmas, because this year you promised to renovate the kitchen, and, of course, the house needs a new roof, and the old tin lizzy is looking especially shoddy compared to the new models just reaching the showrooms.
- Chances are that, left to your own devices you will not implement a financial plan that you paid for. The key phrase here is *left to your own devices*. If you have used a (flat) fee-only planner to design your plan, once the plan is done and the planner paid the fee, there isn't a lot of incentive for that planner to help you implement the plan (unless, perhaps, a further fee can be negotiated). You could be left on your own at a time when you truly need help to get you going and keep you going.

  On the other hand, if you use a commission-only planner,

the planner retains a strong interest in implementation because he or she doesn't get paid until action is taken and commissions are earned.

I'll discuss the pros and cons of fee-only and commission-only planning later in this chapter, so no more about this now. But it is my personal feeling that it's probably a very good thing that somebody besides yourself is willing to take an active interest in implementing your plan. Few people will do so of their own volition or at least do so fully and properly.

Using the continuing services of a planner doesn't imply that you lack willpower. It's more a question of an expert giving you a personal, helping hand through the uncharted territory (and the maze of paperwork that is often required) outlined by the plan. Some people don't read road maps very well. So if you plan a long journey you often will take along a passenger who can. That's just common sense.

6. Keeping Track of How You're Doing

This means monitoring your plan regularly. A periodic review. The best plan is one in a computer — yours or the financial planner's. You must check, preferably every 6 months, the progress you have made. If you get off track, either you alter your financial activities to pull them into line with the plan, or you alter the plan so that it reflects what you consider a new reality.

Be careful about altering the plan. Examine first whether you have followed your plan's recommendations properly. If you have but you are off track, then examine external circumstances. If those have changed, you can drop new information into the computer and come up with an appropriate change of direction. Again, that's the beauty of the computer — it can make the changes so quickly and easily, in a few minutes. No plan is written in stone, because changes in your financial environment (such as sudden, raging inflation, or a sickening leap in interest rates) or in your own needs have to be reflected in your plan. Just be sure the changes aren't momentary spikes that temporarily shoot the voltage up and stimulate you involuntarily to make changes you shouldn't. Only change the plan when it really is called for. Then act on it, immediately.

A financial plan (like all other plans) is based on a number of assumptions. The assumptions can be your net worth *today,* your income, the amount you can save, the amount of life insurance and disability income you require, the rates of inflation and interest. It is much like a navigational plan that will help you fly a private plane from, say, Vancouver to St. John's, Newfoundland, in an estimated 20 hours. You assume a certain wind direction and speed, fuel capacity, ground speed, air speed, compass deflection and so on. If you are piloting that plane, or are navigator, you don't wait until the 20 hours have passed to find out whether you've missed St. John's. You are constantly checking your assumptions as you fly to find out if you are on course, and if not, what has caused the deviation from the plan. Have you picked up a tail wind? Are you facing a stronger head wind? Is a side wind buffeting you off course? Are the weather conditions changing? The entire trip, as a matter of fact, becomes a series of adjustments, fine-tuning and further adjustments before you arrive at the right airport. Similarly, you must regularly and periodically analyze and adjust your financial plan or you can be blown right off your intended course.

16

Where Do You Turn for Help?

I mentioned in the previous chapter that you might want to consider using the services of a professional financial planner. I'd like to amplify that recommendation.

There are some 125 life-insurance companies in Canada, perhaps 45 banks and trust companies, a great number of credit unions and dozens and dozens of families of mutual funds. There is a multitude — literally thousands — of investment and savings vehicles offered by these institutions, each with its merits and each with its tax consequences. Choice is a fact of life today and what sets off our society from many others. But choice can bring with it confusion. This is where a planner's computer can be so useful: an individual planner now has available fingertip information on all the different services and products of a multitude of companies, can analyze it and can recommend the best ones to suit your needs.

At my staff-training classes I sometimes compare a client facing the plethora of financial products and services with my wife sending me to the grocery store for some sugar, some butter, some beef, some toilet paper. I get to the store and I find there are more cuts of beef on the meat counter than I knew there were parts of a cow. Even toilet paper comes in about 18 different brands and varieties. There are double-ply, triple-ply, single-ply, biodegradable and you-name-it. If my wife wasn't specific about what brands she wanted I easily get confused. It's not just a matter of price, but of the relative merits of one product over another based on the number of cents per kilo or per pound. If you acknowledge that shopping in a supermarket can be confusing to a person not used to it, double or triple that confusion when you are talking about financial products and services.

I suggest that most of us need help at various times of our lives, and the preparation of a personal financial plan is one of those times. Of course you can do it yourself. Regardless of whether you call on a planner's expertise, it is largely the information that you provide that is used. After all, it is your plan, they are your objectives and goals and it is your life at stake. But chances are a financial planner can offer invaluable assistance because he or she is skilled in the general planning process. Also a planner can goad you into action and recommend alternate courses of action from time to time. And just as important, he or she can provide you with a variety of options to help you achieve your objectives.

How to Choose a Financial Planner

Before you look for a financial planner, ask yourself some questions. The list here, which isn't foolproof or complete, should give you a clue as to whether you need an expert to help you. And remember, using the services of a stockbroker and/or an accountant is not the same as dealing with a personal financial planner.

- Could I be doing better with the money that I am earning?
- Could I improve my money-management techniques?
- Do neighbors or friends who earn about the same as I do seem to be accomplishing much more with their incomes?
- Do I sometimes wonder whether I'm choosing the right investments for my particular purposes, and whether there might be a better way to get a higher return on my assets?
- Do I really want to know what my net worth is?
- Do I have a good idea of where the money I earn is going and where it is not going, every month?
- Am I taking full advantage of income-tax regulations or might I be paying too much tax because I am not familiar with the details of the act? Am I careless in applying what I know?
- Do I have a good overall idea of where I am going financially, where I want to go, and how to get there?
- Are my disability, life, property, car, major medical and other forms of insurance adequate? Do I suspect I am paying too much for any of them? Do I have the right kind of insurance to

cover my specific needs?

- Are the financial advisors I have completely objective, or are they limited in the scope of recommendations that they can make?
- Do I follow the habit of regularly reviewing my financial picture to make sure it is current, up to date and consistent with current tax laws, interest and inflation rates?
- Most important: have I sat face to face with an expert to determine what goals I should establish for myself (and my family)?

If you answer "no" to any *one* of these questions, then perhaps you could consider calling in a financial planner.

You Have to Be in a Comfort Zone

Above all, you must be comfortable with your financial planner. You must respect his or her credentials, experience and apparent capability. You must be personally comfortable with whomever you choose — that means talking the same language because you'll have a lot to say to each other. It is advisable that you interview 2 or 3 prospective planners before you settle on one. Be satisfied you have chosen the best person available to do the job, and someone whose personality is compatible with yours.

The Criteria to Apply

Financial planning is a fairly new profession, so far as the middle-income wage-earner is concerned. In fact most provinces do not yet regulate the precise function of financial planning. Almost anybody can hang up a shingle as a financial planner or "financial consultant," and some less-than-qualified individuals do. In the United States more than 22,000 investors lost at least $400 million to incompetent or fraudulent "planners" during a 2-year period ending in mid-1988. The problem does not seem to be as extensive in Canada. Some provinces are looking at ways to regulate the industry but it is no easy task to come up with appropriate accreditation criteria. So don't count on it for a while. In the meantime you can't afford to delay.

If you apply 2 main criteria to the potential planners you interview, apart from personality, your chances of finding a good one will improve. The criteria are (1) his or her credentials and (2) the way he or she expects to be paid.

What's in a Name?

Having accreditation as a CA (Chartered Accountant), a CMA (Certified Management Accountant), a CLU (Chartered Life Underwriter), an MBA (Master of Business Administration), a registered stockbroker or mutual-funds salesperson does not make a person a financial planner. A financial planner might well have a background in one or more of these fields, but he or she definitely must have training and preferably experience in the specific field of financial planning.

There are three designations that indicate qualified personal financial planners: (1) CFP, (2) RFP, (3) CH.F.C.

A CFP is a Chartered Financial Planner. This is a designation awarded by the Canadian Institute of Financial Planners for successfully completing a 2- to 3-year correspondence course. The course is a practical one and, in fact, you might want to consider taking it to advance your financial education. Those actually using CFP designation, however, must have had at least two years work experience in the field.

An RFP is a Registered Financial Planner. An RFP does not necessarily have a CFP designation but has had at least 2 years' practical experience as a financial planner, has passed a 6-hour examination set by the Canadian Association of Financial Planners, and has submitted a sample financial plan as proof of proficiency.

A CH.F.C., a fairly recently developed credential, is a Chartered Financial Consultant. The holder is a registered life-insurance agent who has successfully completed financial-planning courses set by the Life Underwriters Association of Canada.

As I mentioned, many individuals connected with the financial-services industries pass themselves off as financial planners. To stack the odds in your favor of finding the perfect planner, however, you should stick to somebody who has at least 1, and preferably more, of these 3 financial planning designations (or is studying toward the designations and is responsible to an accredited supervisor). The various associations in question will provide lists of members if you ask for them.

A word of caution: A planner is somebody with a knowledge of planning. Do not confuse a planner with an investment counselor. The right types of investments become *part* of a personal financial plan, but only a part. A stockbroker, for instance, advises you about investments. But unless that broker has academic and/or practical planning experience, you should shy away so far as planning is concerned. The same goes for an insurance agent or mutual-funds salesperson without planning credentials.

Paying for Planning: Count the Ways, and Be Wise

There are 3 ways that financial planners are paid. Which method they use is one of the first things you should determine when you interview your candidates: (1) fee-only basis, (2) fee-plus-commission basis, and (3) commission-only basis.

Fee-for-service financial planners may charge a flat fee for a complete plan or charge an hourly fee based on the number of hours required to do the job. In general, fee-for-service practitioners are well skilled in the planning process and quite often have backgrounds as chartered or certified general accountants or chartered financial analysts. Some trust and/or life-insurance companies have financial-planning departments and usually are fee-based. Credit unions are starting to get in on the act as well, and they often charge a fee. Most fee-for-service planners also carry the CFP or RFP designations, or both.

Some in the industry see the objectivity of fee-for-service planners as an important strength. This type of planner only recommends financial products to clients — no selling is involved — and therefore, it is assumed, has no financial stake in any particular product and won't be influenced by a company or product source. But since you often require financial products to implement your plan, you must then turn to a stockbroker, mutual-fund and perhaps life-insurance salespeople, and even trust companies or banks for the products to implement your plan. This means you could end up paying a fee for the plan as well as commissions or fees for the products themselves.

Fee-for-service plans tend, though not exclusively, to be beyond the ability of the average wage-earner. Hourly rates for qualified planners range from $80 to $125. You might be able to buy a minimal computer-based plan from a company for a few hundred dollars, and this would include no further, ongoing service. Custom-designed plans, which are the most useful, can run into many thousands of dollars. These would include some degree of continuing service and monitoring. Unless you are in the top few percent of wage-earners, or have assets of at least $250,000 of investment capital, a fee-for-service financial plan likely will be on the rich side for you.

Some financial planners offer both fee-for-services and commission-only plans. I personally feel that planners should not combine these compensation structures with a client, but should quote one way or the other and clearly set out which method they are using.

If you use a commission-only planner, your plan actually costs you nothing. The planner is paid through commissions realized when buying financial products to implement the plan on your behalf. There is, of course, the potential problem of objectivity or the lack of it when a planner's compensation comes from commissions, bonuses or fees paid on the products purchased to implement your financial plan. This is where you have to tread a little carefully and use your judgment. Obviously, the more products and the more financial services companies and sectors your planner represents, the greater are his or her chances of maintaining objectivity. For instance, if your financial planner is licensed for life insurance only, there is always the chance that this may influence the plan's recommendations. The same could hold true for a planner who is a mutual-funds salesperson licensed for that particular product line alone, or for a trust company without direct access to mutual funds or life insurance (and thus no commissions).

Some financial planners do have access to a multitude of products and financial sectors, but because they operate alone they cannot maximize their commissions unless they place the lion's share of their business with one particular company in one particular sector. And if you hire an individual planner not affiliated with an organization of sizable scope, you have to ask what would happen to the servicing of your plan if your planner left the industry, moved, retired, or died. For that matter, what kind of service could you expect if you were to move to another city a thousand miles away?

Ideally, if you use a commission-only financial planner, your best bet is to choose one connected with a national organization so you can expect continuing service from them in another location if you are transferred. The organization should also be large enough to represent a wide range of financial suppliers from all possible financial sectors.

Some General Comments About Making a Choice

The objectivity of most financial planners is usually pretty good. But you also have to use your judgment to assure yourself a planner won't be biased in his or her planning approach because of previous training or discipline. Even some very good chartered accountants can take the position that tax reduction is the sole purpose in life, and inadvertently produce a lopsided plan oriented primarily to reduce tax. So, get to know your potential financial planner, and seek the personal recommendations of friends and acquaintances who may have dealt with a particular planner.

Incidentally, not only commissions can bias a commission-only planner. A planner might receive other considerations from a financial-products supplier and you would never know about them. Free trips to exotic locations for placing a lot of business through one particular company is an example. Or special computer support, office space or equipment.

So, how do you make the best choice? For one thing you ask a lot of questions. For another, your financial planner should belong to a reputable organization that has a code of ethics with teeth in it. Teeth means that failure to uphold that code would mean loss of membership. That helps to assure you of suitability and objectivity in your plan's recommendations.

Be hard-nosed: ask for details on paper. Have your planner give you a disclosure letter outlining specifically the method of compensation. Make sure that all compensation is covered — including all the direct and the indirect compensation received from supplier companies. A good financial planner with nothing to hide will divulge this information in detail. And you have to be tough about getting the information you need to make a proper judgment. Remember, a good financial planner is priceless and a poor financial planner is costly. Until there are appropriate and standard provincial regulations governing this new industry, you have to accept the ancient adage *caveat emptor.* You as the buyer must beware. Don't hesitate to tell a financial planner you want to see accreditation on paper. Check the degrees and schools, the honors bestowed, the associations he or she belongs to. Ask for a copy of whatever code of ethics the planner subscribes to.

In the last analysis, while a financial planner is there to help you formulate goals and implement a plan to achieve them you yourself will have to do most of the work. You (and your family) will have to give a lot of thought to what you want out of life and what your specific goals should be. Don't simply follow what somebody else tells you that you ought to do or must do. You must be an integral part of the financial-planning process all the way down the line, including implementation. Remember this:

- No one, no matter how good he or she is or how objective and no matter how altruistic, is as interested in your financial future as *you* are.
- Few financial planners can be experts in every sector of financial services or taxation. Sometimes planners are only as good as the advisors they have on staff or have available to them. Good financial planners tend to act as the catalysts for a financial plan and they call upon outside experts such as chartered accountants, lawyers, insurance people, real estate people, investment advisors and the like.
- In the end you are going to have to become your own financial planner. The initial plan is merely the start of the process. Your planner should help you become more aware of various financial services, tax and pension legislation, where pertinent. There are myriad courses and seminars you can attend to familiarize yourself with what you have to know over a period of time. Never forget that it is your life and your financial success at stake.

As with most other endeavors in life, your well-being is ultimately your own responsibility. This book is designed to help you to become more familiar with the financial planning process and some of the major areas to consider. But don't ever let a single book be the be-all and end-all of your education. *The Money Jar* is a primer and a primer only. There is much more to learn.

Learning more about financial planning should be your personal adventure, and you should have fun doing it. And the more you learn, the better prepared you will be to provide yourself and your family a future of financial freedom.

17

It's Never Too Late to Start

Where does all this leave you, if you have left it rather late to start saving? Perhaps your circumstances changed radically and suddenly — unexpectedly widowed or divorced perhaps — forcing you to start building up funds for retirement for the first time in your 40s and 50s. Don't despair, it's never too late. The facts of life are that you might never attain the same level of savings as those who started in their 20s or 30s, but you should still be able to get enough together to leave you far better off when you no longer wish to work.

There are 4 things you can do to help make up for a late saving start:

1. Save a higher percentage of your income than a younger person might.
2. Take slightly greater risks when investing your savings. This assumes, reasonably, that the greater the risk, the higher the potential return.
3. Delay retirement and continue working for a few years more to give you time to build up more savings.
4. Plan a second career that will earn you income after retirement.

The obverse of saving is spending. Often we don't have much to show for a lifetime of work, not because saving is so difficult, but because spending is so easy. The week I wrote these words I talked long distance with a chap in Vancouver. He was 51 years old and apologized for the fact that he had accumulated very little capital over the years. He said the reason he hadn't was because he had made some bad investments. (I can't tell you how many clients have said to me, "I don't have much money because I made some bad investments.") When I pressed him further he admitted that whenever he did manage to save any money he soon spent it rather foolishly.

I suspected that is the main reason why a lot of people end up dead broke at age 65. It's easier to admit to making bad investments than to confess that you sold the house for a nice tax-free capital gain and then blew the profits on a new wardrobe, an imported sports car and a trip around the world.

Forget What You Haven't Done, and Get On With It

If you haven't saved much by the time you are age 40 or 50, it won't help to cry over spilt milk. But you'd better start *right now* to save whatever you can. And think about putting aside 20% to 40% of your income each year.

Is it possible to do that? Sure it is. It probably means that your standard of living is not going to improve dramatically, say, between the ages of 45 to 65, because you'll be slicing off a large chunk of your income and salting it away. But you can't have everything. Looking at the situation coolly, there is no question that it is better to make the sacrifice now rather than when you are 15 or 20 years older and have fewer options regarding income.

You can ease into it if your resources are limited. Say you are earning $30,000 a year right now. You immediately start to save 10% of your income — $3,000 a year (that's $250 a month, or $115 every 2 weeks). Next year, when you get a raise, perhaps to $31,000 or $32,000, add that extra $1,000 or $2,000 to your savings instead of buying a new car. Now you are saving up to $4,000 or $5,000 a year.

Assume that you can repeat this exercise for the next 15 years of your working life. At the end of that time you may be earning about $50,000 a year and saving about $20,000 to $23,000 a year. The same applies to the self-employed: don't blow every extra-large commission or the profits from a particularly lucrative sale. Put away as much as possible and don't bump up your living standard.

I admit that 40% is a large proportion of your income. You might well ask yourself how in the world you can do it, knowing full well that your living expenses will continue to rise because of inflation. It's pretty tough to escape the effects of inflation, but remember that you probably have paid off your mortgage by the time you start your savings program. Or if you have children, they should be gone from home. With those 2 prime expenses out of the way, you will find it much easier to save, especially if you are prepared to forgo improving your standard of living.

It's well worth the sacrifice now. And there is a substantial by-product of tightening the purse strings for the next decade or so: if you have been used to living on $30,000 or so a year, you will only need a pension or retirement income of somewhere between $20,000 to $30,000 a year. So you will have disciplined yourself and your expectations to remain within your grasp.

Consider the contrary. You spend your increasing income as the years go by and build up your standard of living to a high level. If you are earning $50,000 or $60,000 when you retire and you have been spending it all, you'll probably need $40,000 or $50,000 a year in retirement income. And the amount you should have saved to create that kind of income is considerably higher than if you were satisfied with $25,000 (in today's dollars) a year in retirement.

There Is a Happy Medium

Is it too much to expect that you won't spend at least some of your increasing income on yourself as you earn it? Perhaps there is a middle way. You could allow yourself a slight improvement in your living standard as you go along and still put some savings away. You probably won't save enough to derive a satisfactory retirement income, but you could plan to apply alternatives (2) and/or (3) and/or (4) (see above) as well to augment your savings.

Whatever you do, you must plan for it and do it now. The alternative you choose depends on your attitude toward life and your ability to sacrifice today for tomorrow's need. You and your spouse, if you have one, must make that decision mutually, and immediately. If you need help to sort out the various possible scenarios, call in a good financial planner. One of the things you can expect of a planner is that he or she will help you work out on paper, usually with the help of a computer, exactly what will happen if you proceed with different sets of variables.

Less Sacrifice Today = More Risk Tomorrow

Suppose you have decided that you can't make the total sacrifice. You will start to save immediately, but you'll also spend some of your annual increases on yourself. That's not an unusual choice. Nor unintelligent. But it does mean you will have to face a gap between what your savings eventually will earn for you and what you will likely need in retirement.

How do you bridge that gap? One way is to invest your savings aggressively. I mean that most of your savings should go into some pretty aggressive growth (equity) plans that could provide you with a return of 18%, 20% or 25% over the years. To do that you have to have a personality that can live with some degree of risk. And that is something you must evaluate before you go ahead. For a proper, and objective, evaluation you should probably have a financial planner test you to determine your propensity for risk-taking or risk-aversion. (See Figure 11.)

RISK-TOLERANCE PROFILE

Please consider each investment goal in terms of your personal objectives; rate that on a scale of 1 to 10, 1 least desirable and 10 most desirable.

1. Safety of Principal	1	2	3	4	5	6	7	8	9	10
2. Investment Liquidity	1	2	3	4	5	6	7	8	9	10
3. Current & Future Income	1	2	3	4	5	6	7	8	9	10
4. Tax Consequences	1	2	3	4	5	6	7	8	9	10
5. Inflation Protection	1	2	3	4	5	6	7	8	9	10
6. Future Appreciation	1	2	3	4	5	6	7	8	9	10
7. Ease of Management	1	2	3	4	5	6	7	8	9	10

How do you rate your tolerance for risk? (please check one)

- ☐ I am very conservative and am more interested in holding on to what I have than in taking risks, even if doing so may make my money grow.
- ☐ I am fairly conservative but am willing to accept some risk in return for potential growth.

- ☐ I can accept a fair amount of risk in exchange for the possibility of having my money grow substantially.
- ☐ I am willing to risk losing some or all of my money if I am convinced that the investment has a chance of paying off big.

Figure 11: This questionnaire helps ascertain a client's capability of handling investment risk.

These tests can pretty well peg what kind of person you are compared to the population as a whole. If you are thinking of investing your savings any way but conservatively, you definitely should be tested. It would be ridiculous (and irresponsible) if you were to adopt an aggressive investment plan and you couldn't sleep at night because of it. If you get insomnia every time the market drops half a point then you should look for a different solution, a less risky one. It's a bit like deciding whether to take the back roads or the throughways. You might be the type of person who should give up a little speed for safety.

You Can Balance the Risk

If your personality proves to be middle-of-the-road, that is you can stand some risk but not a lot, you can hit a happy medium between sleep and insomnia. For instance, you could start saving 10% of your income this year. You could gradually increase this to 20% a year as you approach the decade before retirement by beefing up the rate by just 1% per year. You invest what you save in reasonably conservative-growth mutual funds to give you a safety net. At some point along the way, perhaps after you reach the 15% saving level, you stop building the safety net. In the years following, you use your 1% increase in savings per year to buy really aggressive growth stocks. So now you have some conservative and some risk investments. If the risk investments don't work out, then at least you've got an assured income from the conservative ones. In other words you are not gambling your entire income. A financial planner with a computer can help you do a lot of "what if" thinking so your decisions will be based on reasonably firm ground.

Less Sacrifice Today = Work Longer Tomorrow

Consider the third alternative on the list on page 205 — extending your working life to age 67 or 68. Delaying retirement by just 2 or 3 years doesn't sound like a big deal, but it can make a whale of a difference to your retirement plans. Your investments have more time to accumulate and compound. You could make additional contributions to your RRSPs. And, of course, you would have 2 or 3 more years' worth of savings. And because you and your spouse, if you're married, will be 2 or 3 years older than most people when you retire, you'll probably get a better return from any annuities you might eventually buy. Even delaying your Canada Pension Plan for a couple of years will mean higher payments. (See Figure 12.) Again, a

DELAYING RETIREMENT 2 YEARS CAN PAY OFF

Amount available to buy annuity at age 65: $100,000

Monthly annuity income**	$1,017.98
Canada Pension Plan income**	556.25
Total monthly income	**$1,574.23**

After 2 years amount available has grown at 10%/yr to $121,000

Monthly annuity income**	$1,264.68
Canada Pension Plan income*	623.00
Total monthly income	**$1,887.68**
INCREASE AFTER TWO YEARS	***$313.45/month***

**CPP Maximum figures as of Jan. 1, 1989*

***1983 group annuity mortality table @ 10% interest*

Figure 12: If you delay retirement for two years, you could be at least $313.45 richer each month from the growth in your CPP payments and retirement fund alone. Not shown in this illustration would be 2 years' additional savings growth (in and out of a RRSP) and from Old Age Security payments. The income is based on a Life Guaranteed 10 Years annuity.

qualified personal financial planner could help you calculate what these various moves could mean to you in dollars and cents.

Switching Careers: A New Lease on Retirement

The fourth alternative to starting late is to augment your income after retirement by taking on a new job. Many people beyond age 65 continue working as independent consultants, using the experience they've acquired over a lifetime, working for an employer. Some people turn their hobbies into profitable, money-making ventures. Others find that later in life is never too late to go back to school. University evening programs are crowded with adults, some just because they enjoy learning and some who are out to improve job skills. Many self-employed people don't consider 65 a signal to retire anyway, and might well work for several more years.

The point I want to get across is that you cannot afford to lose another day — start saving right now. You cannot replace one second of the time you lose by waiting. Time is like land — they don't make more of it so it will never be cheaper than right now. If you wait until 6 months before retiring to start planning and saving, you're acting like the football coach whose team was losing and who waited until the 3-minute whistle in the last quarter before finding out the score and adjusting his game plan.

Putting together a comprehensive personal financial plan is not the easiest thing in the world to do, especially if you haven't had much money-management experience and you believe you are not the goal-setting type. But it is not terribly difficult either. It really boils down to first admitting that you'd better start doing something to improve your financial situation. Then you can begin to foster the common sense and self-discipline to work toward financial independence. Hundreds of thousands of people have done it.

If you need help planning, that help is readily available. The cost can be minimal, even nil. And certainly insignificant compared to the benefits. So, there's really no excuse to wait. You're only here once, as the old saw goes, and you can't come back a second time to rectify the mistakes you made and seize the opportunities you missed the first time around. Now that you have read *The Money Jar* you have a golden opportunity to gain control over a vital part of your life: your financial well-being. The result can be exciting and rewarding. I wish you the best of luck following up this particular opportunity!

Appendix

Excerpts of a Sample Financial Plan

This appendix contains excerpts from an actual personal financial plan drawn up for a married couple with two children in a small Ontario town. It is too lengthy to reproduce in full. The plan consists of 40 pages of text and financial tables, some of them computer print-outs, the whole divided by indexed separators into 10 sections. Included too are a few brochures from potential suppliers of financial products that could be used to implement some of the plan's recommendations.

I have included the entire summary, which starts the plan off, plus a few introductions to some of the sections below, and most of the investment analysis. These should give you an idea what parts, at least, of an actual plan look like. Included here are:

1. Financial Plan Summary
2. Net Worth and Cash Flow Analysis
3. Capital Needs Analysis
4. Disability Needs Analysis
5. Retirement Needs Analysis
6. Educational Needs Analysis
7. Capital Accumulation Statement
8. Investment Analysis
9. Insurance Policies
10. Investment Products

PERSONAL FINANCIAL PLAN

FOR

JEAN AND ROGER SMITH

CONFIDENTIAL

January 22, 1989

FINANCIAL PLAN SUMMARY

(Jean and Roger Smith)

The following report presents your current financial situation and offers some planning ideas and recommendations for the two of you to consider. This plan was prepared based on information that you provided and on the following assumptions:

Average rate of inflation		6.00%
Anticipated investment yield		10.00%
Assumed life expectancy	Client	90 years
	Spouse	90 years

We would be prepared to do another plan using another set of assumptions if this is required.

Goals/Objectives

- You wish to maintain/upgrade your personal lifestyle.
- You want to balance your budget.
- You want to pay down your mortgage as soon as possible.
- You want to save for retirement.
- You want to assist your children's post-secondary education.

Net Worth Analysis

A full *Net Worth* statement is enclosed for you and your spouse, showing that you are currently worth $229,500. The purpose of this statement is to show both of you how you have arranged the distribution of your assets and liabilities. It examines whether there is a need to reposition your assets and whether your current debts should be consolidated, paid off from other funds available or refinanced. It also focuses on the relative liquidity of your assets. As you proceed through the financial-planning process, your net worth will serve as a benchmark against which progress in reaching your goals is measured.

Cash Flow Analysis

The itemized *Cash Flow* statement shows your income and expenses on a monthly basis. It is essential that your total income exceed your total expenses, because the bulk of your future savings and asset purchases may have to come out of your regular income.

Emergency Cash Reserve

This reserve is an amount that will enable you and your family to maintain your present living standard in the event you are faced with a loss of income or an unexpected expense. It may even enable a person to change jobs, knowing that funds are in reserve to meet a temporary loss of income. How much to keep on hand can vary from 3 to 6 months' net combined take-home pay — in your case from $5,700 to $11,400.

Maintaining too large a balance can be costly because very liquid savings tend to earn relatively low interest. In your case, we recommend that a minimum of 3 months' expenses (approximately $5,700) be maintained.

Banking Services

It is highly recommended that you get a safety deposit box for the safekeeping of valuable documents and possessions such as insurance contracts, deeds, stock certificates, jewelry, etc.

It is advisable that both spouses be signatories on all bank accounts and safety deposit boxes so that in the event of emergency or premature death the surviving spouse has continuing access.

RISK MANAGEMENT

Life Insurance

In order to determine the adequate amount of life insurance protection to satisfy your family's needs, we have prepared a *Capital Needs Analysis* for each of you, copies of which are attached for your reference. From this, you will see that Roger needs insurance protection of $93,448 in addition to the $41,000 already carried and Jean requires $100,000 in total.

Disability Income

In order to have sufficient income during a period of disability arising out of sickness or injury, it is critical that you have sufficient financial resources available to provide that income, whatever the length of time. The *Disability Income Analysis* provided in this plan illustrates in detail your current coverage compared to the minimum resources you would need to sustain a family lifestyle similar to what you now enjoy. It indicates how much more coverage, if any, you will need and the cost involved.

Home/Tenant and Auto Insurance

Although the coverage required may vary from province to province and location to location, it is important to have sufficient public liability coverage for both risks. A minimum of $1 million to $2 million is advisable in the case of auto insurance. In the case of home-owners/tenants insurance, special consideration should be given to replacement-cost rather than current-value coverage. Insurance costs can be affected by your selection of deductible amounts and this should be reviewed on an ongoing basis.

INVESTMENTS

The formula for financial success is systematic accumulation. You must treat your savings and investment program as bills that must be paid on a regular basis. If these "bills" are paid first from your income rather than from whatever is left at the end of the month, the temptation to overspend is considerably reduced.

The basic philosophy of investing generally is to preserve the capital one has, stay ahead of inflation and increase one's net worth. Therefore, an approach to investing would be to look for four factors in your investments:

1. *Safety.* The aim is to preserve what you already have.
2. *Liquidity.* You should be able to convert at least some of it into cash within a short period of time.
3. *Good Yield.* Your money should grow at a reasonable rate after taking inflation and tax into account.
4. *Catastrophe-proof.* Your investments must be protected against unforeseen events that might occur in the future.

Since most investors (small and large) do not do well on their own, we recommend you use professional money management by acquiring carefully selected investment and savings products.

These financial products, such as guaranteed investment certificates and mutual funds, are designed to provide financial services for investors who do not have the time, inclination, technical knowledge or sufficient capital to effectively manage their own financial investments. Each product has a set of investment and risk objectives. This applies particularly to mutual funds.

The choice you make depends on your financial circumstances and personal preferences.

PLANNING AND SAVING FOR YOUR CHILDREN'S EDUCATION

While it is true that all parents have great ambitions for their children, only a handful of parents actually set up a plan to help insure young people's future security through access to higher learning. The analysis of the educational needs for your children included in this plan shows that the setup of a systematic monthly savings program on an ongoing basis will ensure children the opportunity of going to university or college at a time chosen by them.

RETIREMENT PLANNING

You have indicated that if you received $3,000 per month retirement income, in current dollars, this would be adequate for your retirement needs. We have done extensive calculations using the present value of your retirement fund of $239,500 added to the value of long-term assets to be liquidated at retirement. We have assumed that these funds will earn an average yield of 10.00% and will be exposed to an average inflation rate of 6.00% and that you will live until age 90. Our analysis indicates that you will have to save $297 per month until retirement in order to reach your desired income goals.

TAX PLANNING

It is important to remember that when you are doing tax planning, not all your income is taxed equally. Certain types of income are given tax preferences whereby they are either taxed at a lower rate, tax is deferred or tax not levied at all.

- Income described as capital gains or dividends is taxed at a lower rate than interest income.
- Contributions made to your retirement program are tax deductible and these funds and whatever they earn will only be taxed when they are ultimately withdrawn.
- If you plan in advance, it is possible to generate more after-tax income in your hands.

WILLS AND ESTATE PLANNING

In the absence of a properly executed will, your estate may be distributed as required by law rather than in accordance with your wishes. As well, protection for your heirs should be reviewed and updated by your legal advisor on a regular basis.

IMPLEMENTATION

- Draw up a revised cash flow analysis after taking your new set of expenditures and savings targets into account.
- Target an amount to be saved monthly for the Emergency Cash Reserve.
- Assess total amounts needed for special needs, goals or objectives.
- Maximize contributions to your RRSP.

- Consider investments in mutual funds.
- Purchase required life and disability insurance coverage.
- Consider the tax and estate planning to be done.

We will be glad to assist in fully implementing your financial plan.

Here are a few introductory statements from some sections of the sample plan, and in some cases, the financial tables that back them up:

CASH FLOW AND NET WORTH STATEMENTS

The world we live in is changing rapidly and continuously. What we want from our lives also is continuously changing. Money management provides the means for us to achieve all our financial goals and objectives.

The first step is to learn about how we make financial decisions and to understand our current financial status. Once this is known, good spending habits and strategies can be developed.

The *Cash Flow Statement* (Figure A1) provides a profile of your current income sources and lists all monthly expenditures. This allows you to identify areas where existing funds could be managed more effectively or how they can be applied to obtain specific financial goals.

Unfortunately, most people think of income as their only financial goal. In reality, what we are worth is in many ways far more important than what we earn.

The ultimate goal of financial planning is to ensure that personal goals are met by accumulating sufficient financial resources or net worth.

The *Net Worth Statement* (Figure A2) that follows provides a summary of your current financial situation by itemizing your assets and obligations and your present net worth.

The status of capital you might need in the event of an emergency is also highlighted in the review of your present liquidity.

CAPITAL NEEDS ANALYSIS

The *Capital Needs Analysis* (Figure A3) allows you to establish the exact amount of protection that you and your family require in the event of your death, based on your own specific circumstances.

CASH FLOW STATEMENT
JEAN & ROGER SMITH

INCOME	Monthly Amount	Percentage Total Income
TOTAL INCOME FROM EMPLOYMENT	1,900	80.4%
TOTAL INVESTMENT INCOME	464	19.6%
TOTAL INCOME FROM ALL SOURCES	2,364	100.0%

EXPENSES	Monthly Amount	Percentage Total Expenses
BASIC EXPENSES		
Housing	881	40.8%
Food	400	18.5%
Clothing	300	13.9%
Transportation Expenses	216	10.0%
Telephone	20	0.9%
Recreation & Club Membership	33	1.5%
Personal Insurance	100	4.6%
TOTAL BASIC EXPENSES	1,950	90.4%
TOTAL DISCRETIONARY EXPENSES	207	9.6%
TOTAL MONTHLY EXPENSES	2,157	100.0%
EXCESS or (SHORTAGE)	207	

Figure A1: This is a final, combined cash flow statement. It brings together, in abbreviated form, information contained on 2 separate, preceding income and expenses sheets (not shown) which contain more detailed breakouts of the various income and expense categories.

NET WORTH STATEMENT
JEAN & ROGER SMITH

ASSETS	Amount	Percentage Total Assets
LIQUID ASSETS		
Cash	8,000	3.0%
Short-Term Deposits	7,000	2.6%
TOTAL LIQUID ASSETS	15,000	5.6%

INVESTMENT ASSETS		
Bonds	8,500	3.2%
Real Estate Investments	200,000	74.2%
RRSP	31,000	11.5%
TOTAL INVESTMENT ASSETS	239,500	88.9%
PERSONAL ASSETS		
Art, Antiques, Collectibles	5,000	1.9%
Automobiles	10,000	3.7%
TOTAL PERSONAL ASSETS	15,000	5.6%
TOTAL ASSETS	269,500	100.0%

OBLIGATIONS	Amount	Percentage Total Obligations
SHORT-TERM OBLIGATIONS		
TOTAL SHORT-TERM OBLIGATIONS	0	0.0%
LONG-TERM OBLIGATIONS		
Mortgage – Residence	40,000	100.0%
TOTAL LONG-TERM OBLIGATIONS	40,000	100.0%
TOTAL OBLIGATIONS	40,000	100.0%
NET WORTH (Total Assets–Total Obligations)	**229,500**	

Figure A2

CAPITAL NEEDS ANALYSIS
ROGER SMITH

INVESTMENT INTEREST RATE : 12.00%
INFLATION RATE : 6.00%

CURRENT LIQUID ASSETS		
Life insurance coverage	41,000	
Curront valuo of RRSP	31,000	
Stocks and bonds	8,000	
Other assets	17,000	
TOTAL CURRENT ASSETS		97,000
CURRENT LIABILITIES		
Final expenses	7,500	
Home mortgage	40,000	
Emergency fund	9,000	
TOTAL CURRENT LIABILITIES		56,500
LIABILITIES OVER ASSETS		–40,500

MONTHLY INCOME ANALYSIS

	Dependency Period	Independent Period	Retirement Period
Income Objective	2,500	2,500	2,500
Spouse's earned income	1,300	1,300	0
Government benefits	501	303	691
Other income	450	450	450
Total Income provided	2,251	2,053	1,141
Income shortage	249	447	1,359
CAPITAL REQUIRED	22,263	24,701	86,984
TOTAL CAPITAL REQUIRED			93,448

Figure A3

The analysis includes a summary of your current financial situation and the income needs during the different periods of the lifecycle. The insurance coverage you provide for your dependents or heirs in the event of your death will go to cover the following types of expenses:

- Funeral expenses and an emergency fund to pay current taxes and obligations.
- Funds to pay off the mortgage.
- Educational funds for your children, if applicable.
- An income to cover ongoing living expenses.

In developing a risk-management plan, it is important for you to determine the financial needs of your dependents and the amount of assets that will be liquidated in the event of your death.

RETIREMENT NEEDS ANALYSIS

In Canada, we have the opportunity to work and earn money, but based on current statistics we have not been very successful about accumulating a sufficient amount to retire independently.

After having worked a lifetime, this is the status (according to Statistics Canada 13-206) of individuals over 65: 11% have annual incomes less than $5,000; 62% have annual incomes less than $10,000; 79% have annual incomes less than $15,000. The median income of all individuals aged 65 is $8,525.

One of the most important aspects of the financial-planning process is preparing for a financially secure retirement. Planning for retirement requires a long-term commitment that should not be delayed.

The purpose of the *Retirement Income–Needs Analysis* (Figure A4) is to help you establish a realistic income objective for your retirement, based on today's values, and then to calculate the necessary monthly investment needed to realize the funds required to provide that income at retirement.

RETIREMENT INCOME - NEEDS ANALYSIS
JEAN & ROGER SMITH

SELECTED RETIREMENT AGE : 60
CPP BENEFIT ELECTION AGE : 60
INVESTMENT INTEREST AGE : 10.00%
INFLATION RATE : 6.00%

	Current Dollars	Inflated Dollars
MONTHLY RETIREMENT INCOME GOAL	3,000	12,876
ESTIMATED RETIREMENT INCOME GOAL		
From CPP/OAS	380	1,632
Fixed Income	0	0
Indexed Income	0	0
TOTAL ESTIMATED RETIREMENT INCOME	380	1,632
MONTHLY INCOME SHORTAGE	2,620	11,244
AMOUNT OF CAPITAL NEEDED TO FUND SHORTAGE		2,155,190
ESTIMATED VALUE OF INVESTMENTS		
Retirement Plans		581,744
Real Estate		1,083,471
Stocks and Bonds		86,678
TOTAL ESTIMATED VALUE OF INVESTMENTS		1,751,893
CAPITAL SHORTAGE AT RETIREMENT		403,297
MONTHLY INVESTMENT NEEDED TO FUND SHORTAGE	**297**	

Figure A4

By planning for your retirement today, you minimize the long-term risk of reaching retirement with resources that are inadequate for you to realize the lifestyle you desire at that time.

EDUCATIONAL NEEDS ANALYSIS

For individuals with children, funding education may rank high on your list of financial priorities emotionally, but from an economic perspective it may come last. The reasons for this are twofold:

- Lack of financial and investment flexibility
- Loss of control over assets transferred to children

Nevertheless, guidelines developed for granting financial aid to students place the responsibility of paying educational costs jointly on students and their families.

Typically, university or college costs consist of the following major items: tuition fees, books and supplies, room and board, transportation and personal expenses.

The analysis that follows provides you with an estimate of educational costs you will incur when your children enter university or college, based on today's costs adjusted for interest and inflation. Also shown is the amount of monthly deposit or single deposit required to fund the amounts needed.

Naturally, not all children go to college or university. If they don't they will have a cash reserve available to them and your children will have an advantage in seeking employment, getting specialized training, getting married, having children, buying a home or starting a business — all good things that require money.

INVESTMENT ANALYSIS

Above-average investment results can be obtained if you know your investment objectives and if you allocate the time to evaluate and monitor your investments on a systematic basis.

In formulating an investment strategy, consideration must be given to a number of important factors including not only your age, responsibilities and investment objectives but also your tolerance for risk.

The following concerns should be evaluated:

- Safety of principal
- Liquidity of investment
- Current and future income tax consequences
- Inflation protection
- Future appreciation
- Ease of management

After you have considered these objectives and concerns, you can determine their importance to you. This will provide you with a basis for making sound, ongoing investment decisions.

The next step is to evaluate your present investments. These are summarized in the analysis that follows (Figure A5) along with recommendations, if applicable, for changes to your investment portfolio consistent with your investment objectives.

INVESTMENT ANALYSIS
JEAN & ROGER SMITH

EXISTING PORTFOLIO

Investment Name	Existing Amount	Annual Deposit	Pretax Growth Rate %	After-tax Growth Rate %	Risk Factor
TERM DEPOSITS	7,000	0	10.00	7.50	1
CANADA SAVINGS BONDS	7,000	1,000	9.50	7.13	1
RRSP — BANK —	31,000	2,000	10.00	10.00	1

ACCUMULATED VALUES

	Year 1	Year 3	Year 5	Year 10
TERM DEPOSITS	7,525	8,696	10,049	14,427
CANADA SAVINGS BONDS	8,570	12,054	16,051	28,820
RRSP — BANK —	36,300	48,543	63,357	115,468
TOTAL VALUE	52,395	69,293	89,457	158,715
TOTAL RISK FACTOR	1.00	1.00	1.00	1.00

PROPOSED PORTFOLIO

Investment Name	Existing Amount	Annual Deposit	Pretax Growth Rate %	After-tax Growth Rate %	Risk Factor
TERM DEPOSITS	7,000	0	10.00	7.50	1
CANADA SAVINGS BONDS	7,000	1,000	9.50	7.13	1
RRSP — BANK —	31,000	2,000	10.00	10.00	1
RRSP FIRST CITY	21,000	2,000	14.00	14.00	3
TRIMARK SELECT FUND	5,000	1,000	15.00	12.49	3

ACCUMULATED VALUES

	Year 1	Year 3	Year 5	Year 10
TERM DEPOSITS	7,525	8,696	10,049	14,427
CANADA SAVINGS BONDS	8,570	12,054	16,051	28,820
RRSP — BANK —	36,300	48,543	63,357	115,468
RRSP FIRST CITY	26,220	38,955	55,505	121,941
TRIMARK SELECT FUND	6,749	10,930	16,221	36,430
TOTAL VALUE	85,364	119,178	161,183	317,087
TOTAL RISK FACTOR	1.77	1.84	1.89	2.00

Figure A5: The investment analysis shows the Smiths' current investments and compares them with the recommendations of the planner — and the estimated effect of those recommendations. The planner's changes, after 10 years, would result in a portfolio twice the value of the Smiths' should they carry on without a plan.

Risk and Types of Investment Products

LEVEL 1 — VERY LOW RISK: Cash, savings, GICs, T-Bills, government bonds, life-insurance cash value.

LEVEL 2 — LOW RISK: Corporate bonds, annuities, pension plans, selected RRSPs.

LEVEL 3 — MEDIUM RISK: Residence and other real estate, mutual funds, mortgages, art and antiques, precious metals, rare coins and stamps.

LEVEL 4 — HIGH RISK: Stocks, limited partnerships, business interests.

LEVEL 5 — VERY HIGH RISK: Commodities, tax shelters.

OVERALL SUMMARY

1. Your net worth is $229,500.
2. Your cash flow statement indicates you have $207 over and above your expenses each month.
3. You need $5,700 in an emergency fund.
4. Jean needs $100,000 life insurance.

   Roger needs $105,000 of additional life insurance. This is slightly more than our *Capital Needs Analysis* calls for, but the inflation rate assumption we used in that calculation is perilously close to reality, and it may not be long before reality outstrips the assumption.

   As well, you need to cover the mortgage liability remaining on your rental/income property until it is paid off — it is not now covered by mortgage insurance.

   I recommend universal insurance, which has both protective and savings components.
5. Roger needs $880 per month of disability insurance.

OVERALL RECOMMENDATIONS

1. Reduce your short-term deposit to $6,000 for your emergency fund.
2. Buy the required insurance. This can be done by placing a $100,000 ABC Company policy on Jean with a Child Protection Rider to protect the children. Cost: $592/year or $54.02/month.
3. Buy a $100,000 term life policy on Roger. This protection will be needed only for about 10 years (until the children are on their own). This is the least-expensive way to obtain needed coverage. Cost: $276/year or $25.19/month.
4. Buy disability insurance for Roger. An amount of $880/month

protection would cost $65/month.

5. Reposition your current RRSP investments as follows:
   a) Put $10,000 in the highest interest-bearing guaranteed 5-year term deposit (or GIC) — currently 11.75%.
   b) Put $21,000 into the XYZ Company real estate mutual fund. This will give you flexibility and a great deal of security.
   c) Put $5,000 into the ZWX Fund. ZWX Inc. has one of the best track records in the industry. Your investment should stay well ahead of inflation while in a relatively low-risk fund.
   d) Put all future RRSP contributions into the CBA Growth or CBA Equity Fund. Both of these are managed by the RSQ Corporation. They both have 10-year track records of 18% average growth, and the company's management team should assure a consistent performance.

I hope these somewhat disjointed segments have given you an idea of what an actual personal financial plan is like on paper. I can assure you that the entire document has a logical continuity that makes it easy to read and understand.

Whether you do your own planning or use a professional planner to help you, I know you will find the process an exciting one. And profitable to boot. Happy planning!